Contents

New Journeys Now Begin

Learning on the path of grief and loss

Tom Gordon

WILD GOOSE PUBLICATIONS

www.ionabooks.com

Published by
Wild Goose Publications
4th Floor, Savoy House, 140 Sauchiehall St, Glasgow G2 3DH, UK
www.ionabooks.com
Wild Goose Publications is the publishing division
of the Iona Community. Scottish Charity No. SCO03794.
Limited Company Reg. No. SCO96243.

ISBN 1-905010-08 7
13-digit ISBN 978-1-905010-08-0

Cover photo © Mary Gordon

A catalogue record for this book is available from the British Library.

Overseas distribution:
Australia: Willow Connection Pty Ltd, Unit 4A, 3-9 Kenneth Rd,
Manly Vale, NSW 2093
New Zealand: Pleroma, Higginson Street, Otane 4170,
Central Hawkes Bay
Canada: Novalis/Bayard Publishing & Distribution, 10 Lower
Spadina Ave., Suite 400, Toronto, Ontario M5V 2Z2

Permission to reproduce any part of this work in Australia or New Zealand
should be sought from Willow Connection.

Printed by Bell & Bain, Thornliebank, Glasgow, UK

To Jean and Jimmy, Mary and Willie,
Talbot, Farquar, Colin and countless others,
whom I loved in their living and still grieve for in their dying,
but who are part of every new journey I will ever travel.

Acknowledgements

I suggested in my acknowledgements for *A Need for Living* that writing a book was like giving birth – inasmuch as any man can understand what that means. Well, the child I bore and gave birth to these few years ago is now, it would appear, standing on its own feet and able to make its way in the world, largely independently from me. That process, and the helpful comments from many people, has given me the encouragement to offer another infant child to the world. But this time I do so with more confidence, knowing that this new life has an older sibling to stand beside.

I am immensely grateful to many people for their support in the preparation of this book: my wife, Mary, for her unfailing patience and love - and for the photo from the North End of Iona which graces the front cover; my colleagues in the hospice team, particularly Alice and Mairi, from whom I have learned such a lot and with whom it is a pleasure to work in our bereavement support service; Ann, for the space and time she gave me in Fife; Sandra, Alex, Neil and Tri at Wild Goose Publications, for their patience, reassurance and thorough professionalism; Eric Bogle, for the wonder of his music and his ready willingness to allow a phrase from one of his songs to be used as the book's title; Tom Fleming, for his graciousness in agreeing to write the foreword, and offering the profound insights with which this book can begin; all those who have agreed that their stories could be offered to a wider public; and others who have given permission to use quotes from books and song lyrics.

But most of all I pay tribute to the people whose stories, insights and growth give this book its contents and purpose. They would never consider themselves to be in any way special, far less wish their names and circumstances to be readily identified. Through the years, they have been trusting enough to allow me to offer what support I could in their bereavement journeys, but they, in return, have given me much more than they will ever know.

Tom Gordon
April 2006
Port Seton, East Lothian

Foreword

by Tom Fleming

This impressive, informed and intensely moving book by Tom Gordon makes an important contribution to a subject of universal relevance. Death and bereavement are experiences shared at some time by all of us. My generation has often been guilty of pushing these stark realities beyond the horizon of daily consciousness for as long as possible. For me, having an awareness of death is not to be afflicted by chronic morbidity. It is what gives to every moment of life an unrepeatable wonder and joy. Death is not the mystery. Life is the mystery and the miracle.

Perhaps I am lucky that such awareness came to me early. I was four and not yet at school when my mother, a skilful artist and a young woman of forty, full of love and fun, died, unexpectedly, from complications after surgery. I was present when my father, a Baptist minister, was told of her death by our family doctor. It was the first time I had seen a grown-up cry. In the custom of the time my mother's body rested in the front room of our house. When I was taken in to see her I was intrigued to find a familiar face looking as if it was sculpted from whitest marble. I stretched out a finger to see if the skin on her brow still moved – and was unceremoniously hustled from the room. Rows of chairs arrived by van for the funeral service, also held in our home, but when the day of the funeral arrived my older sister and brother were allowed to stay and I was packed off, despite my vehement protests, to 'play' in a neighbour's garden.

It was forty years later, while visiting Australia to perform at the Adelaide Festival, that an elderly friend of the family handed me a letter written by my father in the days immediately following my mother's death. It read, 'We are all devastated by our loss. Fortunately wee Tommy is too young to understand.'

These words taught me a great deal about received attitudes to grief. You can live in the same household and be unaware of or unresponsive to feelings which do not match your own. I was 'too young' but I did understand that my mother had died and that her going would leave an unfillable gap in all our lives. I was 'too young' but I did understand that I didn't want in some way to be 'shut out' because of that. I was 'too young' but I did understand that for the distant (and mostly unknown) relations who appeared in our house to eat ham sandwiches after the funeral it wasn't as important an event as it was for me. It was just that my reaction was not the accepted norm among 'grown-ups'. For me death was in J.M. Barrie's words 'a great adventure' – a totally new and interesting experience. The small child lacks the sentimentality of the adult and the child mind can be quite clinical in its insatiable curiosity.

That experience prepared me for a succession of family deaths, culminating in my father's death from a long-standing heart condition when I was twelve. That was the end of home-life as I had known it. We lived in a manse so, on my father's demise, my sister and brother and I had to move out within a couple of months. I left for school one December morning never to return to the house where I was born. Others decided what few possessions we could retain. We moved to my elderly grandfather's house on the south side of Edinburgh. A year later he died and we had to move again. Then my sister married and left for England, while my brother joined the Fleet Air Arm (it was war-time) and served mainly overseas. I continued my schooling living in 'digs' until that was completed.

You may gain the impression from all this that my formative years were dogged by misfortune and filled with gloom. Nothing could be further from the truth. I was left with an overwhelming sense of deep gratitude for having had such wonderful parents, for spending my earliest years in the happiest of homes and for the ongoing kindnesses of so many friends in the years since. If I have inherited one legacy of mixed blessing it is a fierce independence of spirit - a character flaw I am still trying to deal with on the eve of my eightieth year!

As one grows older, acquaintance with grief sets one on an ever steeper learning curve. Friends from childhood, valued colleagues from working adventures and, more painfully, those who have shared one's life most intimately (and, therefore, know one best) are with increasing frequency removed from the scene.

Familiarity with such events doesn't make them easier to bear. I had got tickets for my closest friend and his wife to attend the opening night of *King Lear* at Stratford in November 1962. A couple of hours before 'curtain up' I had a telephone call to say he had died of a heart attack, aged 54, in a London hospital. The anxiety and fear which accompany a first night performance in the theatre saw me through, until, in the last minutes of that epic tragedy, came the words: 'Why should a horse, a dog, a rat have life, and thou no breath at all?' That eternally questioning word 'WHY?' ... One comes to realise that, often, what we mourn is that part of ourselves which seems to have gone for ever and that what those we love have meant to us lives on, woven into the very stuff of our daily being.

In more than half a century of describing national and state occasions for the BBC, including historic funerals both at home and overseas, I always tried to remind myself that, under the panoply of solemn ceremonial, this was a time of deep emotion for some individual human being on whose personal grief we were intruding. Each year at the Service of Remembrance at the Cenotaph, confronted with the appalling statistics of war, I was at pains to try to ensure that a younger generation did not simply count the cost of human folly in millions, but would come to understand that each of these millions had a name, was, for the most part, young and had dreams and hopes for a future that was denied to them.

Tom Gordon's splendid and enlightening book is a treasury of understanding, wisdom and insight into the nature and complexity of grief. Much of his understanding has come from his years as a hospice chaplain. His wisdom comes from appreciating that everyone who comes into his care is unique, and from sharing with us, honestly and openly, the insights which stem from his own personal encounters with grief and loss. He is sustained in his relentlessly demanding work by a profound Christian faith and a dedicated sense of vocation, neither of which he uses as a 'weapon'. Above all, he listens. I hope he may hear the words 'Thank you' that all readers of this book, myself included, will surely wish to speak from the depths of their hearts.

Tom Fleming

Introduction

'Anyone can stop a man's life, but no one his death;
a thousand doors open on to it.'
Seneca: 'Phoenissae'

'Winks hard, and talks of darkness at noonday'
William Cowper: 'The progress of error'

The idea for this book has been in my mind for a long time. Even before I wrote *A Need for Living* I had been feeling that while much has been written about theories of grief to help with an understanding of loss, the material best suited to those who are experiencing bereavement is about people who are themselves bereaved. Whether a newspaper article by a celebrity reflecting on the death of a partner, a glossy magazine interview with someone coping with a tragedy, a diary of an individual's thoughts and insights, or a pamphlet of recollections, it is the experiences of those who are bereaved that are the most helpful guides for others in that situation.

The response to *A Need for Living* served to reinforce this perception. Readers have been gracious enough to share with me their reactions to the people, stories and issues in the book. They tell me that they can relate to this person or that, identify with one event or another, or place themselves in one or more of the circumstances outlined. They can understand and work with one of the images offered. They can use the prayers, poems and reflections as a guide to their own thinking. And so, as a consequence, they feel less alone, knowing that someone out there has gone down a road before them and understands just what they are going through. Their problem isn't 'magicked' away and their journey doesn't become miraculously straightforward. But they now have someone or something to relate to. So they feel less isolated as they learn to live with their new feelings. They tell me they have been helped as a result.

In addition, those who work with people who are living with loss – whether in a family context, with friends or colleagues, or in the caring professions – have indicated that reading about people and their circumstances in that first book has enabled them to understand more readily what the individuals they are caring for are going through. As a consequence, they have been better equipped to offer insight and support in helping them on the unpredictable journeys of living and dying.

So it is to real individuals and real stories that people turn in their distress and anguish to find the kind of help and understanding that theories and theorists will never be able completely to fulfil. My conclusion, therefore, is that more of this needs to be offered in the areas of grief and loss.

Indeed, I have come to believe that this is all the more necessary in a society which gives us so little time to grieve following a death. Friends, work, communities, even family, give us too little time to mourn. Between six weeks and two months seems to be the norm (so different from the 'widow's weeds' and the 'year-and-a-day' of mourning in a past age!). After that we are expected to function normally. It isn't that people don't care, or don't ask, or don't support. It isn't that we don't know that bereavement issues go on for a long time. It's just that the world rushes on and doesn't have the patience or the time to be tolerant for too long with us and our loss, or indeed even to remember how recent our loss might have been.

As a consequence, therefore, we are given too short a time for our public grieving. And in buying into that, for mostly we have no choice, we learn to function and relate to our society as best we can. We learn – in a sense for our own survival in a society such as ours – to live double lives. On the one hand we hold down the job, attend functions, go to church, organise the family home, or whatever. We even tell people we are fine when they ask. We play the role of someone who is coping OK. We live the necessary, expected public life. And, on the other hand, we keep our sorrow private. Who ever knows that we cry ourselves to sleep? To whom do we speak of the pain of going into an empty house? Who ever notices the extra make-up that hides the pale and drawn face, or the stiff upper lip that is clearly a mask to our feelings? (And if anyone does, would they ever say so?) Who is aware of the little moments of memory that reduce us to a puddle on the floor? Very few, if any, I suspect. So we become more isolated in our grief, with no norms against which to measure our feelings and no context in which to check out our journey of loss. That role is a desperately lonely one. We try our best to learn to live with pain and sorrow, but who knows or cares?

So in this double life we have to become adept at playing these two roles. People will even say – with a sigh of relief – 'How brave he is, and back to work so soon. He's so loyal to the Company.' 'She's doing very well, you know, don't you think? And so soon after her husband's death.' 'What a great example he is. What a faith!' 'I saw her at the school with the grandchildren the other day. They must be a godsend to her' - as people in their loss are held up as examples of stoicism, and coping, and faith, and getting-back-to-normal, and all those positive characteristics we so much admire. Acting that role has done its job. Society doesn't have to worry about us any more, for it sees what it sees and asks no more questions.

But the other role? – the real one? – who knows about that? Who *really* knows what we are living with? Whom do we tell? Who will accept the brokenness and the weakness when the mask slips and the other side is revealed? We don't even like it ourselves, far less have it accepted as the norm by others. So, who is going to reassure us that we are acting out this other role with equal normality and skill?

I spoke with Jack while I was writing this introduction. Jack had been through a bad Christmas, the second since his wife had died. Many people had told him that once the first year was out of the way and he'd gone through everything once, that was the hard bit over. Now things would get steadily better. But the second Christmas without Sally was worse than ever, and the fact that he had expected it to be better 'made the worse even worse', he told me. And through his tears he shared this painful but profound insight: 'I've come to realise that the pain doesn't go away. That big void is still there. You never stop grieving. You just learn different ways to hide it.' Only, this Christmas, he couldn't hide it any more, and thank God he was prepared to tell someone how it really was.

As William Cowper suggests[1], no matter how hard we might wink and put a brave face on things, we will also have to face our darkness at noonday. Or as the ancient wisdom of Seneca[2] tells us, we cannot stop a death, 'a thousand doors open on to it'. That is the given. Like Jack, we will all experience the darkness of 'the world of man' and our loss will be black. Why then should we not recognise that we are fellow travellers with those who are bereaved and that we and they are simply facing one of the thousand doors that open on to the same inevitability of death? Why then should people facing bereavement and being overwhelmed by grief not be able to hold out a hand that will be grasped by others who understand and can help? Why are we not ready to offer support because we know that this is what happens to people in the isolation of their loss? Why do we not begin with the recognition that the blackness of loss, and the depth of feeling that loss creates, are absolutely understandable? In our pressurised, immediate and impatient society, is it not all the more important to offer to people who journey with loss the companionship of those who accept and understand what they are living with? Is it not essential to travel with them for a while in the reality of their journey, and so help them feel less alone?

Over my eleven years as a hospice chaplain I have been a part of our hospice's bereavement support team. This support structure offers a framework providing the 'checking out' context so lacking in our present society. As a consequence, it addresses the over-whelming sense of isolation people feel in their loss, and therefore helps them to accept and understand their experiences. It isn't being too dramatic to say that it offers some people companionship in their loss which they don't appear to be getting from anywhere or anyone else. I'll say a little more later about the structure and value of the way our bereavement support service operates. But two specific things have become clear to me as that work continues. Firstly, I greatly value my opportunity to work with bereaved people. Indeed, I find it one of the most rewarding and stimulating facets of my job. And secondly, the people with whom I have worked, who constantly amaze me with their insights, resilience, coping mecha-nisms and powers of regeneration, have important stories to tell which can and should be a help to others. Such people may not feel themselves to be special and their journeys of loss to be in any way extraordinary. They may never be able to offer their insights to a wider audience. But they have the kind of stories that people 'out there' need to hear. For having found the value of companionship in their own journeys of loss they can, in the telling of their stories, offer companionship to those who have no access to support struc-tures, and who may therefore feel increasingly confused about their feelings and more alone in their losses.

In addition, I have had my own losses to work through. I'll share some of these stories too as the book unfolds. That means, therefore, that some elements of this book will be autobiographical. But that's the way it has to be. For to become detached from the pain and sorrow integral to the dying process and the bereavement journey, or to find some magical inoculation which will protect us from the hurt in what we hear and share with those to whom we offer companionship is, I believe, to cease to care. So working through my own losses and being touched by and learning from the losses of others are two sides of the same coin, and they continue to offer me insights into the bereavement process.

In my hospice chaplaincy I know with certainty that if we offer compassion to those who are dying, in the real companionship dying people crave, healing can be found in the face of mortality. So it is with the journey of bereavement. Now, I am no Classicist! I scraped O-Level Latin in high school, and Mr McGregor – of blessed memory – would be astonished that anything of his teaching still remains. But I know this much - both compassion and companion begin with the same prefix, from the Latin 'cum', meaning 'with'. What people who are hurting need above all else is for us to be 'with' them in their pain – as Sheila Cassidy writes in *Sharing the Darkness*[3]: 'Sometimes sitting empty handed when you would rather run away.' We cannot be there and say we are fully involved without some of the hurt and pain slipping under our defences. It goes with the territory. If we have seen death through one of the thousand doors, then surely we must know our own 'darkness at noonday' and feel the same feelings and have to deal with the same issues. We are constantly challenged, therefore, to look at our own journey, face our own demons, and find reconciliation with our own losses. Some of these lessons learned have been the most important of my life. I offer them to you because they still mean so much.

But mostly I'll be a storyteller, sharing the tales of people I have met and worked with throughout my life, both in recent years in my hospice chaplaincy and from experiences that have left indelible traces on my soul from my previous twenty years as a parish minister. In my stories I'll bring real people to life again, hold up real insights and offer real companionship and help. Some of these people will know that their stories are being shared with you. Some have had their names and details altered so that they can remain anonymous and still have their story told. Some accounts are amalgams of a variety of people and circumstances whose stories come together around a common theme but whose identities should never be known. But all these people have known loss, and they all have something important to say.

While the idea of the book has been in my mind for a while, the title around which the ideas have crystallised is very new. As a present for my 54th birthday, my daughter Mairi took me to a concert in the Edinburgh Fringe, where we were entertained by the wonderful singer/songwriter Eric Bogle, a long-time favourite of mine. A native of Peebles in the Scottish Borders, Eric left Scotland in the late 1960s to settle in Australia – one of the many 'ten-quid tourists' who emigrated at that time. The writer of such songs as 'The band played Waltzing Matilda', 'Leaving Nancy' and 'Willie McBride' (also known as 'The Green Fields of France'), Eric writes and sings with insight and passion about life, injustice, hypocrisy and love.

In a great concert, Eric Bogle sang old favourites as well as new songs. Introducing one of his new songs, he told the story of the first time he came back to Scotland after emigrating. He and his father had never got on too well, but now, back home a more mature man, Eric found that things were better between them. Sadly, his father died a short time later, so the new beginning of a growing relationship was cut all too short. After his father's death, Eric set himself the task of scattering his father's ashes on his beloved river Tweed which runs through Peebles. The feelings and insights of that event and, through it, his deep reflections on his relationship with his father gave Eric a song he penned nearly thirty years later. These are his words, and I am grateful for his permission to reprint them here[4].

How clear the river runs
Beneath the noonday sun,
Through trees it twists and turns
In light and shade.
In the Summer's warm embrace
Nature flaunts her bonny face;

A more green and peaceful place
God never made.

On the river bank I stand,
My father's ashes in my hand;
I'm there at his command,
One promise left to keep;
Though in my mind the past appears
A sad parade of wasted years.
Grief and guilt both fuel the tears;
At last I weep.

And there's anger in my heart;
It's bitter, deep and dark.
But for whom or for what
It's hard to tell.
Is it for blind, uncaring fate
That builds bridges far too late?
For his life, for his escape,
Or for myself?

But who the hell am I
To discount or deny,
To say what made him laugh or cry,
Or brought him pain or joy?
Early strangers we became,
And strangers we remained,
The man who made his pride his chains,
And the sullen boy.

But this song's been too often sung,
For what's done is long done;
There's little comfort to be wrung

From a past bled dry.
He was what he was made;
The cards he was dealt, he played,
With as much choice in this charade
As you or I.

Without joy, there is no grief;
Without hope, there's no belief;
Without love, Death's just a thief
Who steals nothing more than time.
So with love, I scatter him
To the water and the wind.
Two new journeys now begin,
His and mine

And there was the line – it struck me powerfully then and has remained with me since: 'New journeys now begin'. For Eric Bogle and his father, in practical and metaphysical terms, in living and in growing, there were two journeys. But new journeys beginning, and the learning and the growing which begin when we are bereaved, starting from that life-changing moment of loss, are common to us all. Bereavement is not an illness to be cured, but a journey to be embarked upon. Loss is not a problem to be solved, but a road to be travelled. Grief is not one stage of life to be coped with, but a series of different pathways along which we have to move as best we can. Such journeys are new to those who are facing loss and bereavement for the first time. Such roads are strange. Such pathways are unfamiliar. Such uncharted stages are dark and frightening. But other people have been along them before us and can tell of how they have managed.

Such new beginnings start now. Can we listen to others who tell us how they have begun their journey? Can we learn from the growth of purpose others have found as their journeys have unfolded? Such movement never ends but has new beginnings over and over again. Can we gain understanding from the ebb and flow, the two-steps-forward-and-one-step-back which others have experienced? 'New journeys now begin' as people face up to their losses every day. Such are the people whose stories this book will tell. Such are the journeys of growing and learning that are worth the sharing. Such are the insights which can help others in their loss.

Before I end this story of the beginning, let me share one more background reflection. I mentioned earlier that I have been part of the bereavement support team in my hospice since I began my full-time work as chaplain in 1994. During that time I have shared our bereavement support work with two colleagues, Alice Leckie and Mairi Findlay, Principal and Senior Social Workers respectively on the hospice team. They are great colleagues. Their support and insight and the shared nature of our bereavement support work have been invaluable to me, and I know – because the people who make use of our bereavement support service tell us so – that they have also been of enormous value to people on their journeys of loss.

Quite clearly some of the stories of the people in this book are as much theirs as they are mine. Along with good volunteers, the team itself begins new journeys of learning and growing every time we reflect on a session of our work. Listening to people tell their stories and seeing them grow in confidence as their journeys of loss proceed gives us a sense of reward, a satisfaction that we have had a part to play in the progressing of these journeys. But even more, we know that we have the privilege of continuing to learn about the journeys themselves, their twists and turns, their smooth paths and rough stretches, their signposts and their resting places, and as a result are better able to be companions to others as their 'new journeys now begin' too.

Eric Bogle sings about what we all know – that to love and be loved means we will experience the pain of loss. We will know grief because we know what love means. We understand bereavement because we have given ourselves in love and have known selfless love in return.

Without joy, there is no grief;
Without hope, there's no belief;
Without love, Death's just a thief
Who steals nothing more than time.

Loss and grief are the given, as are love and joy. They walk hand in hand. One can speak to the other. I hope we never stop learning and gaining new insights as loss and grief are experienced. And I hope that the people whose stories this book will tell will help your learning and growing start again here and now, and give you support for whatever new journey now begins for you.

Notes

1 William Cowper (1731 1800), from 'The progress of error'.
2 Seneca (4BC–AD65), from 'Phoenissae', line 152.
3 *Sharing the Darkness* by Sheila Cassidy, published and copyright 1988 by Darton, Longman and Todd, quoted in *A Need For Living*
4 From the CD *Endangered Species* by Eric Bogle, Greentrax Recordings Ltd, CDTRAX 196; lyrics by Eric Bogle; publisher and copyright-holder Larrikin Music Australia; reprinted with permission.

The seasons of grief

Every stage of grief has its season,
And every facet of loss has its time.

A time for disbelief, and a time for harsh reality.
A time to know, and a time to be consumed by unknowing.
A time of clarity, and a time of uncertainty.
A time for public smiles, and a time for private tears.
A time to be thankful, and a time of regret.
A time of giving up, and a time for going on.
A time of living half a life, and a time of wanting to live again.
A time of then, and a time of now.
A time to feel hopeless, and a time to be positive.
A time of looking forward, and a time of wanting life to end.
A time of faith, and a time of doubt.
A time for holding on, and a time for letting go.
A time when steps are light, and a time when limbs are tired.
A time of hazy memories, and a time of instant recall.
A time for living with death, and a time for living with life.
A time of fruitlessness, and a time of growth.
A time of despair, and a time of purpose.
A time of emptiness, and a time of hope.
A time for rage, and a time for peace.

Time

'It takes time,' they said.
'a long time.
After all, time is a great healer.
So you'll need the time.
Give it time,' they said.

'But how much time?' I asked.
'How long a time
will this great healing take?
What time will I be given?
What time does my grief need?' I asked.

'More time,' we say.
'A longer time than people know,
a time for healing of your pain.
You'll know the need of that
given time,' we say.

'In time,' I say,
'I'll know a time to live again.
Be patient with me in my healing.
I need the time it takes.
My time,' I say.

The times we shared
will turn to memories over time.
And longing time,
and missing time,
will ever be my times with you.

Weekends

Oh God, how I hate weekends,
with those huge chunks of days
that seem to go on and on,
and take up much more time
than any endless, wet Saturday afternoon.

Oh God, how I hate the nothingness,
the endless hours to fill
with trivia,
and doing things alone.
It's no fun browsing B&Q by yourself.

Oh God, how I long for Mondays,
(Oh, I never, ever dreamed I'd feel like that!)
another chance
to meet and greet and know
another world
and other people
and other things to focus on
more than my emptiness.

Oh God, how I hate weekends.
And where were you?
Waiting for me on Monday?

One

The depth of relationships

'Ae fond kiss, and then we sever;
Ae farewell, and then forever!'
Robert Burns: 'Ae fond kiss'

'His banner over me was love'
Bible: Song of Solomon 1:4

In *A Need for Living* I tell the story of a niece whose struggle to cope
with the death of an aunt was as difficult a journey of grief as I had
ever come across. At the time of writing that book, I was still working with this very vulnerable woman, and although there were signs
that she was slowly adjusting to being without the most important
person in her life, it was hard to see how and when things were really
going to come right again. I'm pleased to say that, four years on, she
has made it, and life, while obviously very different and remaining
unfulfilled in lots of ways, has begun to take on new meaning and
purpose. Much of that has been through a commitment to charity
fundraising, and many charities have now benefited from her passion
to raise money for people in need. Out of pain and devastation have
come the beginnings of hope and living again.

The depth of the loss this person experienced reflected the depth
of the relationship she and her aunt had in their life together. 'Without joy there is no grief.' Deep grief was inevitable when true joy
ended with the death of a loved one. Aunt and niece, close as they
were in age and drawn together through their need for love and
support, had become inseparable, perhaps unhealthily so. None the
less, their interdependence meant that regardless of who was to die
first the remaining person would feel that all of their purpose in life
had disappeared too.

Over the years I have had presented to me, in parish work, with individuals in the hospice, and in working with groups in our bereavement support service, the all-too-familiar devastation of similar losses. One person's life has become so intertwined with another's that it's as if two lives have become one. So when one half dies, there appears to be no useful purpose for the other. The devastation is total and overwhelming. People talk of hopelessness, of a wish that their own life would end, and there are often thoughts – and sometimes even talk – of suicide. The pain of the loss is so incredibly deep that it is as if the life of the person who is left has also ended.

There's a legend which tells of an elderly married couple who had lived such exemplary, good and righteous lives, and had thus pleased the gods, that they were to be rewarded before their lives came to an end. So the gods offered them their ultimate prize. They could choose anything they wished. There was no limit. They had the whole world to choose from – wealth, fame, knowledge, power: you name it, it was theirs for the asking. So the old couple considered this wonderful offer, and with dignity and care pondered their options. Eventually the time came for their decision to be announced. So they were called before the assembled gods and were asked what gift they would choose above all else. And they told the gods their choice: that they would die together.

I was a young boy when I first heard that old tale, and I thought it interesting but somewhat fanciful. Why would they choose this when there were so many other more interesting things just within their grasp? Why talk about death when life was precious and full of possibilities? Why want to die together, for goodness' sake? But what did I know then about relationships, commitment, lifelong sharing? Obviously not a lot. And, anyway, as a wee boy I was immortal, as all wee boys are. Death and its consequences were not in the forefront of my young and uninformed mind! Life was full and rich and would, of course, go on for ever and ever. But when I hear that old legend now, I can understand perfectly what it means. I know the love I have for my own wife, Mary, and how deep and vitally important it is to us both. And I also know about our mortality. So we have to face the fact that, after more than thirty years of marriage, both she and I will struggle beyond belief when either of us is bereft of our life partner. If the gods were to ask us to choose a gift above all else, I would hope that our response might be the same as that of the old couple in the legend.

More than that, I can understand the old couple's choice when I hear and see and feel the pain of loss in those who are bereaved of the love of their life. When Robert Burns's 'ae fond kiss' is gone for ever with the death, then life simply isn't worth living any more. The devastation is total, and nothing of any worth and value can be seen beyond the loss. I have seen that pain in a young woman whose husband was killed in an accident after six months of marriage. I have seen that pain in a widower whose wife died at the age of 89 after 64 years of marriage. I have seen that pain in a teenage daughter after the death of her father, her hero, her role-model and her best mate. I have seen that pain in an elderly spinster following the loss of her older sister, from whom she had been largely inseparable for the whole of her life.

You will have seen it too, and, like me, you will have been deeply affected by the depth of such grief. It isn't to do with the length of time a relationship has been in place, and it's nothing to do with gender or age or the nature of the relationship. It's to do with the depth of love that has been experienced, the fulfilment such love has given on both sides, and the fear and hopelessness that is left when the tie of love is severed. So let me tell you in more detail the stories of two very different people, how they came through their struggles with loss, and some of the important insights they have to share.

Glenda was a delightful woman who from time to time came to

worship in my church. I was on 'good morning' terms with her, but I got to know her at a deeper level when her husband died. Death had come after a short and traumatic illness, and the confusion and bewilderment of Glenda and the family was as expected as it was difficult for them all. They dealt with the funeral well enough, because it was about focus and planning and having things to do and think about, the obvious and necessary start to the grief process where real feelings are so often masked or temporarily overcome by 'keeping ourselves busy'. But it wasn't until two months or so after the funeral that I began to realise what Glenda was really living with. She was 58 years old, and she and Clive, her husband, had been happily married for just over 33 years. Clive was a lawyer, and, as the years had gone by, he had built up not only a very successful business locally, but also a reputation in government circles relating to the field of European law. Glenda and Clive lived a comfortable, though not ostentatious, lifestyle. Glenda didn't have to work and she saw her role as a support and companion for her husband. She travelled with him. She sat with him at official dinners. She hosted necessary cocktail parties. She socialised at important functions. She organised his travel, and supported him on lecture tours and at the presentation of important papers and seminars.

Glenda and Clive were inseparable. Holidays were a much-needed respite from the pressures of work. But a deep love and commitment to the whole of their life together was the sustaining feature for them both. They had one daughter, Jennifer, who lived abroad, and who, like her father, was a career lawyer. Unmarried, she was close to both her parents, though circumstances meant that they didn't meet up as a family very often. E-mails and phone-calls were vital tools for their ongoing contact. And then, of course, there was retirement – the great god of retirement. Clive had decided he would retire at sixty. After all, there would be no financial worries, and, with more time together, he and Glenda could 'live off the fruits of their labours' and do all the things together they had always wanted to do. Trips to see their daughter were already being planned. A plot had been chosen on which to build that longed-for house in the country. Talking of those often-hinted-at night-school classes in water-colour painting and basic Russian, and doing them together, had made them feel quite young again.

Nine months before his sixtieth birthday, Clive saw his doctor about persistent headaches which, although he had put them down to stress and 'not being as young as I used to be', had become more troublesome in recent times. Tests diagnosed a brain tumour. Within six months he was dead. Glenda was devastated. Though she was left comfortably well off, that counted for nothing against the loss of her whole reason for living. The new journey beginning for her was one which she did not expect or want. The road she and Clive antici-pated in retirement had been an idyllic pathway down which they would stroll hand in hand into the sunset of life, together, in love, living happily ever after. But the road she had now been forced to travel was a much rougher one, a strange and uncertain road with no signposts, no clear destination, a road with dark and frightening stages, and she was travelling it absolutely alone. 'Ae fond kiss' had been shared in love often enough – oh, the joy of those moments! – and the promise had been for ever. But now the farewell of death had destroyed that promise. The partnership had been severed, and it was permanent.

In the depth of Glenda's loss she is no different from the rest of us. We know that we have no control over life and its twists and turns, and we know that we will not live for ever. But our hopes and desires often become such a clear focus for us, and our plans and ideas so important, that they almost become real. They take on a life of their own, and as a result we think they will rescue us from the trials and tribulations, and grind and sacrifices of life thus far. And so often the promise of retirement is the wishing-well into which we throw the silver coins of our hopes and dreams, believing that our wishing should, and will, become reality. But when these dreams are inextricably tied up with our love for another person, and that person dies before our hopes are fulfilled, then our wishes are denied and all that had stretched out before us dies too. Our hopes and desires, our wishes and dreams, are gone for ever. Something that had already become real for us is snatched away.

For Glenda, there was anger too. It was a strange yet fundamentally understandable feeling, and in her case it was mostly directed at Clive. She didn't want to feel this way, but she simply couldn't help it. Clive had promised her so much, and now he had abandoned her. He had been her mainstay, and now he had left her alone. He had been her reason for living, and now he had gone, and he had taken all the good stuff with him. And, boy, was she angry! It was an anger that she knew was irrational – she knew Clive had not chosen to go, that he had been the victim of an illness that was not of his making, that he would have not have done her harm by choice. But if the longest journey in the world is between the head and the heart, what Glenda's head knew her heart did not accept or understand. The heart that was broken was ferociously angry at the pain of loss, and the anger was directed at the one who had caused that pain.

I could have said to Glenda, 'But you were never promised the future anyway. Why didn't you live in the present and appreciate what you had? (Carpe diem, and all that ...) Why did you put so much faith in a scenario that wasn't yet real? Why did you put all your eggs in one basket in the hope that it would all come right later on? Does the loss of the future diminish the value of what you and Clive had together?' and much more besides. But to have begun to say anything of the sort at the beginning of her journey of loss would have been unhelpful. It would have served to push her away, and deny her the right to feel what she was feeling. And what would that have achieved but to isolate her further in her loss and make her feel that nobody had any understanding of her circumstances?

All these kinds of thoughts were in my mind as I worked with Glenda through her loss. But to air them, and, even more, to throw them at her as a way of insisting that she rationalise things and 'move on', would have been to dismiss the depth of her feelings. It was necessary to understand the nature of her grief. She did not need judgement about how she and Clive had handled things, but she needed someone to help her see that a future, a different future, was possible. Glenda had to find an understanding of her loss. She had to begin with her anger at Clive for promising her so much and then abandoning her before he could deliver. She needed support to cope with the loss of her hopes and dreams as well as the loss of her husband. And, above all, she needed help to come, in time, to celebrate the love she and Clive had had together, the love that remained very deep, but which could now no longer be expressed in physical terms.

The depth of Glenda's loss was a product of the depth of her relationship. The banner of love had been placed over the profound commitment that had given Glenda and Clive their reason for living. Now Glenda was grieving out of the depth of love she had known. Is that so strange? Do we not grieve because we have loved so much? But what are we to do - choose not to risk giving ourselves in love because we fear we may have to cope with the pain of loss? If that is our choice, we will be so protective of ourselves, so afraid of pain, that we will not love at all. What kind of life and fulfilment would that offer us?

Love carries with it the inevitability of loss. One day my wife or I will have to face the death of our lifelong partner. For myself, I cannot even begin to anticipate what that will be like. I know it will be painful. I know my heart will be broken. I have no concept of how I will cope. Yet would I have given up the chance to have shared love with Mary over all these years because the pain of death would be hard? I think not. 'Without joy there is no grief'. Without love there is no loss.

Kate Rusby[5] writes wonderful lyrics, and sings them with exquisite beauty. The words of this song seem to sum up for her the loss of love. I don't know the background to the song. But for me her words encapsulate the pain of the loss of a loved one, and the accompanying sense of impossibility of starting again without them. I'm grateful for Kate's permission to print them here.

You hear me shout when no one's about,
You find me where I can't be seen,
I feel the air flowing, for life's in full swing,
So tell me why I cannot breathe?

Here I am falling, oh why am I falling?
Take me to where I belong.
I'm standing here falling, before you I'm falling,
If it weren't for your wings I'd be gone.

Time moves on and time won't be long,
In time I will fear not the day.
I'm endlessly knowing that you'll never know
What I might want you to say.

Here I am falling, oh why am I falling?
Take me to where I belong.
I'm standing here falling, before you I'm falling,
If it weren't for your wings I'd be gone.

My back it aches, my body it breaks,
To grow my own wings I have tried.
Painless I came, now aimless remain,
Alone and adrift on the tide.

Here I am falling, oh why am I falling?
Take me to where I belong.
I'm standing here falling, before you I'm falling,
If it weren't for your wings I'd be gone.

So we shout when no one's about lest we admit to the pain of our grief, not wanting other people to know the depth of our sorrow. We are unable to breathe when everyone else is flowing along in life's full swing. Yes there will come a time when we stop hurting and fearing each new day as it comes, but for now the endless not-knowing threatens to overwhelm us. Our body aches. We fail to grow the wings that will sustain us when other wings, the wings we really want, the ones that have sustained us for so long, have gone. We feel aimless, directionless, adrift on the tide, not knowing how or when life can be good again. And we fall, again and again we fall, and in falling we stumble along, and in falling we hurt, and in falling we wonder if we will ever make it. 'I'm standing here falling,' we cry. But who will listen? Who will care? Who will understand? This was where Glenda had to begin her journey of loss.

The pain of loss which results from such deep relationships is not, of course, confined to the death of a husband or wife. I have already mentioned a niece struggling with the death of an aunt, such was the closeness the two women had shared over many years. How often have I heard 'Wind beneath my wings'[6] played at a funeral service because the father, mother, son, daughter, husband, wife had been the special person who had given meaning and purpose to another's life, and, as a result of that love, the pain of loss was so deep?

Such is the story of Steve. Actually, the story begins with Grant, whom I had come to know through church circles. Grant was a regular soldier, married young and divorced for some years, who was now dying of cancer. He was a delightful man in his early fifties and was well supported by a faithful mother and two older brothers.

Steve was Grant's best mate. They had met in the army, and though Steve was now in civvy-street and working in advertising, they had remained best friends. Holidays, leisure time, days off were all shared together. And, now that Grant was dying, Steve was a regular visitor at his bedside.

One day when I was visiting Grant in hospital, Steve was there. It was obvious that the friendship was very deep, and that Grant greatly appreciated Steve's company. I didn't stay long. The depth of their friendship was more important than a minister's visit. But as I was leaving Steve followed me to the door of the room. 'Can I come to see you sometime?' he asked. 'Of course,' I replied, and an arrangement to meet was duly made. When Steve and I sat down together the following day, he shared with me a most beautiful story. He told me he and Grant were gay, that they had formed a relationship in the army which had deepened into a loving partnership. While Steve had 'come out' following his discharge from the army, Grant had not. He was fearful of the reactions of his colleagues. He could not face the response of his mother and his brothers. Although they were good people and hugely caring of Grant in his dying, he had decided some time ago that he could not tell them, and indeed, as far as I am aware, he never did.

So Grant and Steve had kept their relationship secret. On days off, Grant stayed at Steve's flat. All their spare time was spent in each other's company. They loved each other like neither of them had loved before. And now that Grant was dying, Steve was devastated. Steve had nowhere he could exhibit the public side of his grief. To do so would be to 'out' Grant and to make his dying more difficult. Thankfully, he had some good friends who understood. And I was grateful he had been trusting enough to share his story with me. He made me promise I wouldn't share this with Grant, and I never did. Grant and I spoke often of the importance of Steve in his life. He never told me he was gay. Maybe he never needed to. The affirmation of the value of the relationship appeared to be enough. Grant died peacefully a few weeks later, having been comforted along the way by lots of love and tender care. And he died when Steve was visiting on his own and when they were holding hands together. There is a God after all!

But if the process of Grant's dying was hard for Steve, the bereavement journey was even harder. For if he could not be public about his fears as he anticipated the loss, how could he be public about the depth of his sorrow in bereavement? When your partner, the love of your life, has died and there is no opportunity for a public expression of that, what are you to do? When you have to sit at the back of the church and not with the 'chief mourners'; when your name is not mentioned along with 'those who have loved Grant the most'; when a whole part of a life is not recognised in a thanksgiving prayer for the person who has died, what are you to do with your sorrow? Such were Steve's dilemmas and pain, and such was the isolation of his grief.

I have long believed that the gift of love is not defined by gender or social conventions. It is what it is: a gift, not sought or found, not bought or achieved. It is a gift to be cherished like all gifts, with a gratitude for the love of the giver. I believe that love in all forms is a gift my God is pleased to give to his children.

So I worked with Steve as later I was to work with Glenda, acknowledging the depth of his relationship and the consequent depth of his grief, made worse in his circumstances by the enforced privacy of his loss. Occasionally we prayed together. Sometimes we wrote to each other. Often we exchanged e-mails. From time to time we met and talked some more. Slowly, Steve began to move on, because, I believe, we started with an acknowledgement of the depth of his loss out of the depth of his relationship with Grant.

One thing we did, as I recall, was to revisit the pain of the funeral. Of course we could never 're-enact' the funeral service so that it would become right for Steve and would contain something of his and Grant's loving relationship. What was done was done. Yet we had to find ways of being true to his cherished memories of the relationship shared. Grant and Steve had loved walking the Scottish hills together. So Steve decided he would take himself off into the Borders and go on a favourite walk. He took with him a little gift Grant had given him − he never told me what it was − and a letter he'd written to Grant. High up in the hills, he went slightly off the path and in a quiet spot with a glorious view he buried the gift and the letter, made a little cairn of stones, and sat and wept. But the tears were good tears, he told me. They were tears of completion, of thanks, of prayer and of blessed memories.

There are times, of course, when the heavy burdens of living cause a person in the hopelessness of life, or in the often protracted process of watching a loved one die, to welcome death - 'the poor man's dearest friend'[7]. Death often comes as a blessed relief. But for most of us, the more common experience is to face the horror and offence of death and to struggle unwillingly with the consequent oppression and mourning. We love life. We hate death. We mourn the people who are gone because we have loved them, and we hate the mourning that their parting from us brings. Glenda and Steve know that as they continue to live with their losses. But they know it because they also understand that we were made to love - Glenda and Clive, Steve and Grant − and Mary and I know that too.

My wife will tell you that I could never be described as an 'incurable romantic', but thankfully she knows what I know, that our love is precious and deeply cherished. And I also know what she knows, that death with all its horror and devastation cannot and will not threaten or destroy our love. 'Death is destroyed; victory is complete! Where, Death, is your victory? Where, Death, is your power to hurt?'[8] So, even this non-incurable-romantic knows what these romantic words of Alfred Lord Tennyson really mean[9]:

What time the mighty moon was gathering light
Love paced the thymy plots of Paradise,
And all about him roll'd his lustrous eyes;
When, turning round a cassia, full in view,
Death, walking all alone beneath a yew,
And talking to himself, first met his sight:
'You must begone,' said Death, 'these walks are mine.'
Love wept and spread his sheeny vans for flight;
Yet ere he parted said, 'This hour is thine:
Thou art the shadow of life, and as the tree
Stands in the sun and shadows all beneath,
So in the light of great eternity
Life eminent creates the shade of death;
The shadow passeth when the tree shall fall,
But I shall reign for ever over all.'

For Steve and Glenda, and countless others in their loss, Love is scared, terrified, indeed, when Death appears, and weeps and spreads 'his sheeny vans for flight'. Yet they now know what others, thankfully, have also come to know in time, that Love can speak again, can stand up to Death, can call it for what it is: the 'shade of death' life will inevitably create, but which one day will pass. In 'the light of great eternity' we will know that Love 'shall reign for ever over all'.

Steve goes back from time to time to visit Grant's cairn and commune with his loving partner. Glenda's daughter, Jennifer, got married last year and it was a very happy day. So, even those who grieve deeply out of the depth of their relationships move on. And Clive was very real at his daughter's wedding. And Grant is very real by a Borders' cairn. The depth of love continues for ever. Death has had its hour, but Love, in all its wonder and joy and healing touch, still reigns.

Notes

5   Written by Kate Rusby, from the CD *Underneath the Stars*, Pure Records 2003, PRCD012. Lyrics reprinted with permission.

6   'Wind beneath my wings', lyrics by Bette Midler.

7   Robert Burns (1759–1796), from 'Man was made to mourn'.

8   1 Corinthians 15:54a–55

9   Alfred Lord Tennyson (1809–1892), from 'Love and Death'.

What to do when someone dies

'You'll find it here,' she said
and handed me the file of which she spoke.
And there it was,
the first of all the leaflets there,
the white,
the shiny one,
which shouted now at me:
'What you should do when someone dies.'

What you should do?
What I should do?
Can any list
define such purposes for me?
Should any leaflet, gleaming white,
tell me what I must do?
I know,
I know what I should do when someone dies,
though never list has ever come my way.

I know –
for deep within me roars
a great ferocious storm
that threatens now to burst with all its violent rage.
I needs must let it roar,
break forth with all its angry power,
and howl and screech
with such destructive force
that no mere world could e'er withstand its might.

What I should do when you have died?
I must let go,
and scream,
and wail,
and curse,
and shake my fists at death.

I know,
I know.
I need no list to tell me so.

'This one,' she says,
'you'll find in here what happens next.
You register the death,
this form
the Doctor gave,
you'll need to do it right.
And other things will help out too,
her birth certificate ...'

Her birth,
her death,
too little time between the two,
but now, forever bound are they
in what I have to do
with Registrar
and you.

'What you should do when someone dies.'
Yes,
yes,
I'll do that too,
I'll do it right.
I'll use your list.
I'll sort it out OK, in time.
And maybe then
when lists are thrown aside,
when shining white becomes a dog-eared grey,
I'll do what I should also do,
and learn to scream and curse
though that was never written down
on any list.

It's Tuesday

It's Tuesday,
and Tuesday is our day to walk,
to walk our favourite path,
and sing
a glorious harmony
that no one else can hear.

This Tuesday,
is my day to walk alone.
A favourite path's a different walk
in silence,
when harmony remains a memory song
with one part missing.

It's August 12th –
our glorious twelfth,
our wedding day,
when hope began,
and lovers' joy sang songs beyond our wild imaginings,
and others heard and joined our choir of love.

This August 12th
who will recall the day it all began?
An anniversary's an awful thing
alone,
when all the anniversaries that have ever been
crowd in on me,
and there's no singing now.

It's Christmas time
with all those endless days
of shallow insight
into Incarnation's joy,

when somehow,
sometimes,
God comes down with Angel songs.

This Christmas time,
all these endless days
speak now of waste and empty celebration.
This Incarnation's failed
when somehow,
often, even now,
my God has died,
and Angels cease their praise.

It's June,
beloved June,
a month that gave you birth
and death,
and cradled you in nurture's love,
and gave you life,
and claimed that life again.

This June,
O dreadful June,
I weep your birth,
I rage your death,
I curse that cradled hope
that took you from your love,
and gave me pain in place of summer's songs.

It's time,
it's days and special days,
it's living with those times

when no one knows but me
what you had brought
of life
and love
and harmonies
and endless possibilities
for me.

This time,
this day,
this special day
is living in each moment
with our endless separation,
to hold again to that which now I know
this day, is mine and yours,
to share again in loving privacy,
and find
this day
the time,
the voice,
to live,
and love
and sing again.

When love is

When love is rich,
Let me not be impoverished by its passing.
When love is bright,
Let me not be overwhelmed by the darkness of its going.
When love is joy,
Let me not be cast down by my sadness.
When love is full,
Let me not be broken by my emptiness.
When love is life,
Let me not be destroyed by dying.
When love is God,
Let me not be rejected by my doubting.
When love is good,
Let me not lose faith in love's own goodness.
When love is you,
Let me not lose love in your departing.
When love is me.
Let me not lose hope for all my living.

Two

Denying reality

'I do not believe in Belief ... Lord I disbelieve – help thou my unbelief.'
E.M. Forster: 'Two cheers for democracy'

'Tout passe, tout casse, tout lasse'
(Everything passes, everything perishes, everything palls)
Anon

No one wants to experience pain. The body has a natural defence against the reality of it –it's called shock. Even the most intense pain may not be felt until the period of shock is over. When I was a young, newly qualified minister, I worked in Easterhouse in Glasgow, a sprawling housing scheme on the city's eastern periphery. Late one night I was on my way home from the church when I came across a crowd of teenagers in a stairwell. This was not unusual of itself, as kids would congregate in various spots well into the night. But this gathering had a different feel to it from normal. As I approached, one of the boys turned to me and said, 'Davie's been stabbed.' And sure enough, when the crowd parted, there was Davie, a lad I knew from the youth club, slumped in the doorway. 'They got me in ma gut,' he said – more calmly that I could have expected – 'right here.' His hands, held over the wound, were covered in blood. 'Has anyone called an ambulance?' I asked the crowd. 'Aye, they're on their way,' someone replied.

For the few minutes it took for the ambulance to appear, I knelt with Davie. He neither moaned nor cried, not just for macho reasons, I realised, but simply because he did not yet feel the extent of the pain. In some fashion – which I confess I do not fully understand, nor have I experienced it myself to prove it to be true – the body, in shock, had cushioned him from the pain. When the ambulance arrived, however, it was a different matter altogether. When Davie took his hands away from the wound and saw the blood, he screamed. When the paramedics lifted him into the ambulance, he was moaning, cursing and shouting. Reality had hit him. The shock was over. The pain was real.

Thankfully, Davie's injury turned out not to be life-threatening. They never found out who had perpetrated the evil deed. Davie knew – as, I suspect, did most of the kids who'd been there that night. No doubt there would have been reprisals, such were the gang battles which even yet bedevil our peripheral and inner-city estates. But Davie? He lived off the kudos of his stabbing for weeks. Moaning and screaming once reality dawned? 'Nae chance!' Never mentioned – though some of us know different.

If such shock can temporarily cushion us from the reality of physical pain, it's not surprising that when someone is told that they have a life-threatening illness, or that their loved one is going to die, or when the news of a death is communicated, people go into shock and refuse to believe the reality. It is too painful to contemplate, too traumatic to be accepted as real. How many times have I watched someone who has heard bad news simply close down, stare blankly, make no sound or movement, as if they had withdrawn at that moment into a cocoon of safety and denial?

Denial was Eddie's reaction, though the shock of hearing bad news manifested itself in a very different way – with no cocoon of safety for anyone! Eddie's sister had died, but, sadly, the family couldn't get in touch with him on the morning of the death to tell him what had happened. We discovered later that he had been on 'a bender' the night before and was unrousable that morning, sleeping off his over-indulgence – a not-uncommon occurrence, we were told. So when Eddie appeared at the hospice early in the afternoon to visit his sister, expecting to be able to see her and talk with her, we were faced with a man who would have to be told, there and then, that his sister had died. When he heard the news he went out of control. 'I don't believe you,' was the first thing he said. 'You're all bloody liars,' he shouted. 'She was OK yesterday. No one said she was going to die. I don't believe you. She can't be dead.' He was ferociously angry, lashing out, swearing at the doctors, scaring even the most experienced of the nurses, and not doing much for the peace of mind of the chaplain either! Eddie was not to be convinced.

Eventually, his brother arrived, and we all tried to help Eddie grasp the reality of what was happening. It became clear that he would not believe us; he would not and could not accept the reality of the death, unless he had the chance to see his sister. By this time she was in our mortuary. If he could only grasp the truth by seeing his sister there, that had to be the way forward. One of the nurses and I had the task of taking Eddie and his brother to the family room adjacent to the mortuary where their sister had been laid out. It took some time to get this organised, and, we were told later, it took all the resources of the staff to keep Eddie calm in this waiting period. When eventually we gathered in the family room, watching Eddie with his sister was as heart-rending a scene as I can ever recall. He held her. He shook her. He shouted, 'Don't leave me, Paula, don't leave me!' He raged and he swore. The reality of the death was too hellish for him to bear. My nurse colleague and I both agreed later that we'd been pretty scared, and that it had been like watching a bad and disturbing movie.

In time, Eddie's brother took him home. I don't know what happened to them next or how they coped. We had no further contact with or from the family. But I suspect it would have taken Eddie a long time to believe the reality, even though he'd now seen his dead sister. I suspect there would have been a bit of hysteria at the funeral service. I suspect that his brother and the rest of the family would have had to struggle with his grief as well as their own. I suspect there would have been a few more 'benders' in the process. I suspect Eddie still doesn't want to believe his sister has gone.

As part of my teaching on issues of grief and loss, I share an exercise with people about losing 'things' before I go on to talk about bigger losses such as redundancy, divorce, and, of course, bereavement. In small groups, and later in the bigger grouping, people are encouraged to share the story of their loss – their keys, wallet, briefcase, car, or whatever – and draw out their reactions to that loss and the feelings that came up for them. The discovery – and to some people a helpful and enlightening revelation – is always predictable, that the feelings and reactions they have experienced and talked about are exactly the same ones that surface when they have to deal with death. And one of the most predominant of these reactions is disbelief. You simply do not want to believe that this loss has happened. The consequences of it are just too great to contemplate.

So, for example, you've lost your car keys, and you will search and search for them with an ever-increasing sense of panic, because the knock-on effect of accepting the loss is too horrendous to get your head round. And how many times in that loss will you return to the place where you think you left your keys, even though you have looked there a dozen times already, just in case you have missed them and they will all of a sudden reappear as if by magic? How often in your frantic search do you hope and, indeed, believe that the keys will just manifest themselves again, and that the loss and all its horrible consequences have just been some kind of bad dream?

So it is with death. Shock and disbelief are normal reactions, for the consequences of accepting the death are too much to take in, too horrible to comprehend. Eddie tried to shake his sister awake to prove to himself that she wasn't really dead. And while this is, thankfully, an extreme and unusual reaction, it's not uncommon for people in their disbelief to go looking for the person who has died, to stare at the chair where they always sat in the hope that the bad dream might be over and their loved one will reappear. A widow told me she had seen her dead husband in the street, and her heart had started pumping with the excitement that he was alive again, because she wanted to believe that the loss hadn't happened and that the bad dream was over.

I'll share a little more on this issue in a later chapter, 'Searching for the spirit', but, for now, let me tell you this story. My wife and one of our daughters recently went to an orchestral concert and I asked my wife later if she had enjoyed it. She confessed that she'd missed most of the first half because there was a man two rows in front who, from the back, was the double of her father, dressed the same, with the same haircut, and with the same mannerisms. And for an instant, her father, who had died a few years before, was alive again. It was, she recalled later, a 'bitter-sweet' experience – sweet because of the depth of pleasure of seeing her father, believing that he was alive again, and wanting to hold on to that moment for as long as possible; and bitter because she knew the moment would pass, and that she would have to live again with the acceptance of his death, with all its accompanying pain. No wonder the first half of the concert went by unnoticed!

Disbelief, and the hope that accompanies it of a re-emergence from a 'bad dream', is a powerfully protective tool. So it is important for those of us who care for dying and bereaved people to understand and accept that it is a perfectly natural mechanism. We have to wait with patience until reality dawns – and has to dawn again and again and again – and still be there when the effect of that reality calls us to journey with those who will cry out, 'I do not believe in Belief.'[10]

People often tell us in our bereavement support groups that, some months after a death – four or six or more months later perhaps – when they thought they'd been 'doing so well', they are now feeling worse than ever – 'like I've gone back to the beginning'. In a sense they have, for what is happening is that reality has dawned, they are beginning to accept the permanence of the death as a fact and they now have to live with it. The 'unreality', the 'bad dream' phase, has come and gone, and the pain and the 'for-ever-and-ever' of the loss is being experienced as very real indeed. No wonder people feel for a time that it is getting worse rather than better.

To use a mathematical image, the graph which plots the improvement in our coping over time is not a smooth, continuous one, even though it may have felt like that at the start. Instead it's a 'roller coaster' graph, even a jagged, unpredictable one. Yes, it still shows improvement over time, but in those 'downturns' in the graph, in those times of 'going backwards', it's hard not to feel that it has all started to go wrong when it had been going so well. And if that is hard for those who are experiencing the low points of their loss, it is also hard for those of us who seek to understand and be supportive. For our patience as carers is sorely tried. We want to see signs of continued progress, and we want to hurry people on to grasp the reality and live with it and work with it and move through it. And our understanding is tested when we, too, have been encouraged and, indeed, relieved by someone's progress, and are now out of our depth when they appear to be regressing.

Lewis Carroll in *Alice's Adventures in Wonderland* has Father William respond thus to a young man's questioning[11]:

'I have answered three questions, and that is enough,'
Said his father, 'don't give yourself airs!
Do you think I can listen all day to such stuff?
Be off, or I'll kick you downstairs!'

So often this is how we are with people whose disbelief makes them unable, or even refuse, to grasp reality, or, when reality dawns, express their pain as being worse than it was before. Perhaps we have to learn to 'listen all day' and wait until the airs of questioning and disbelief dissipate and reality looms through the mist. Perhaps we need to remember that support must be available in the troughs as well as at the peaks of the graph.

Such were my feelings when I was dealing with Peter. His story, in its unfolding, and especially in its conclusion, took me very much by surprise. Peter and Sally had been married for four years. Sally was a thirty-two-year-old who was a patient in our hospice, and Peter, her husband, two years older, was a faithful and regular visitor and an unbelievably important, sensitive and dignified support. The nature of the progression of Sally's illness meant that she was in and out of our hospice over a number of months, with us as an in-patient for two or three weeks to seek control of her symptoms – pain, nausea and the like and then home for a spell to be cared for by Peter, good and close friends, our Marie Curie Community Palliative Care Nurse, and good input from the Primary Care Health Team.

As a result, all of us in the hospice got to know Peter and Sally very well, and it was satisfying to see that, with the input of various members of the hospice team and through the establishing of some deep and trusting relationships, all facets of Peter and Sally's care were well covered, including deep and searching spiritual questions about meaning and relationships and beliefs and God. They had been encouraged to talk things through together and were facing their very different and unplanned-for life and the reality of Sally's death with openness and honesty. Sally had written letters to her lovely nieces who, she felt, though too small to understand the reality of what was happening, needed something tangible from her that they could keep after her death. She had even written birthday cards for them to be given long after she had gone. These were tender times.

Peter, Sally and I had talked about plans for her funeral – and if ever there is a privilege for a hospice chaplain it is to be allowed into the intimacies of the plans and ideas of someone who is giving thought to their own funeral. This is a very important area, and I'll offer further thoughts on a number of aspects of it when I look at 'Rituals and celebrations' in a later chapter.

So, over the months, gently and supportively, good holistic care had been given by all the team. And it was no surprise, therefore, that when Sally came to the terminal stage of her illness, having stayed at home as long as she felt she was able, she decided to come into the hospice to die. Time was now short, to be numbered in days rather than weeks. Peter had taken extended leave from work. Sally and he had a single room together, and, with devotion and tenderness, he played a major part in her care right to the end.

The day Sally died, everyone was well prepared for the end, including Peter. We gave him privacy when he needed it and company when it was preferred. Often the company would be in silence, and sometimes gentle words would be shared. I happened to be in the room when the end came. The scene was loving in the extreme. Peter was sitting close up to Sally by the side of her bed. He was cradling her head in the crook of his arm. He was watching her breathing, talking gently to her, from time to time stroking her brow. The breathing became ever more shallow, until it faded away to nothing, like the dying of a candle flame. And then, it was no more. Sally had gone. It was a beautiful ending.

But I was not ready for what happened next. Peter continued to talk gently to Sally. No surprise in that of itself, for it is not uncommon for people to continue to talk to a loved one after they have gone. But this was different. And, after what seemed to me to be a very long time, it dawned on me that Peter didn't realise that she'd died. What was I to do? Was I to break the moment of concentration and announce the reality? Was I to slip quietly away and leave them together? Was I to blurt out the truth because I felt uncomfortable with what was happening? I decided to stay and say nothing and let the moment run a bit longer. After what seemed an age, Peter turned to me and asked, 'Tom, when do you think she's going to die?' 'Peter,' I replied, 'she's gone. Sally has died already.'

There was what I can only describe as an anguished cry. 'No! No!' he shouted. 'Tell me it's not true. This can't be happening. Sally, Sally, don't leave me.' Here, in a graphic and unexpected scene, was Peter's disbelief. The pain of death's reality was so unbelievable and overwhelming that Peter, like Eddie with his sister, went straight into denial mode – I don't want to, I don't have to feel the pain. If I don't believe it, I won't have to face the hurt.

When Peter had turned to me and asked that surprising question about when Sally was going to die, I remember feeling my own disbelief. Have we not told you? Have we not prepared you for this? Don't tell me you didn't know.

'I have answered three questions, and that is enough,'
Said his father, 'don't give yourself airs!'

I remember feeling my own anger. Are you daft, man? Get real. See what you see. Get a grip.

'Do you think I can listen all day to such stuff?
Be off, or I'll kick you downstairs!'

But he didn't know, and he couldn't accept. At that moment the shock of the death was too much to bear. And when reality dawned, it was obvious why. Of course he knew, as we all do, that 'everything passes, everything perishes, everything palls'[12], but in that moment of loss, knowledge was overwhelmed by denial and intellect superseded by emotion. And all the preparation in the world could not equip this grieving husband for the fact of death and the devastation of his loss.

Often people tell us that when they have had a lot of time to prepare for a death, with dignity, openness and love, 'business has been finished'. Important things have been said and heard, and, in the end, the release and blessed relief of death is welcomed and embraced as right and good. But they also say that, when it happens, they are surprised because it seems as if they'd had no time at all; the reality of death hits them as if it were a sudden car accident or a massive coronary. Thankfully, this is our reality. I say thankfully, for I would never wish personally to be so prepared for a death that I had protected myself in a suit of armour so that I could not feel the hurt. And, hard though it is to watch and be part of, I would not wish that for others in their loss either.

Another incident portrays this vividly. A young husband and father was dying of a brain tumour more quickly than anyone wished and before his wife and the wider family had time properly to prepare the children for the reality of what they would have to face. As a result, in consultation with the family, the option was taken up that the hospice staff should be involved in 'breaking the bad news' to the children. So it was that, in a family sitting room, a doctor, nurse and myself gathered with the three children of the family – Sean, aged fourteen, sitting beside his best mate; his young sister, Karen, aged ten, sitting on the arm of her gran's chair; and wee Stevie, aged seven, standing by the window, devouring a can of lemonade and a packet of crisps – along with their mother, grandparents, and various supportive friends and family members. The time came for the information to be shared. It could not be staved off any longer. So, a very caring doctor, who had worked closely with the family and had already met the children, began the process. 'Do you remember yesterday,' he said, addressing the children, 'when I said that sometimes doctors were very clever and could make people better, and sometimes they couldn't?' There were nods. 'Well ...' He paused. I thought this was pretty good, and that he had stopped to allow the children and the rest of us to catch up with the reality of what would be coming next. He was honest enough to tell me later that he had paused because he simply didn't know what to say. The silence went on for what seemed an age. So I decided something else should be said. 'I think what the doctor's trying to say,' I began, 'is that there's nothing the doctors can do to make your daddy better.' And, after taking a big breath, I used the words, 'That means that your daddy is going to die.' It was one of the hardest things I've ever had to do. I can feel even now how I felt then – sick to my stomach.

However, it's the reaction of the three children which stays with me even more vividly. It took this form. I glanced over at Sean, and saw that his face had gone blank. He just stared ahead, not moving a muscle. A teenager 'being cool' in front of his family and friends? Or a young man cocooned by shock who could not and would not take in what he'd just heard? Then ten-year-old Karen burst into floods of tears and rushed across to her mother and clung to her, sobbing into her shoulder. The horror of what she'd heard? Or reacting to the atmosphere and tension of the room? But most intriguing of all was young Stevie. This wee boy calmly placed his can and his crisp packet on the window-sill, turned his back on the assembled company, stuck his fingers in his ears, and started to sing – in exactly the same fashion as I'd observed many a child in a school playground do when they wanted to block out name-calling from other children. Stevie didn't want to hear the bad news, or the tears and hysterics that followed. 'Block it out!' was his instant response. 'Then I won't have to listen to it at all.'

These three children had reacted to bad news as per the standard textbook descriptions – the stunned disbelief, the bursting into tears, and the blocking out of the news because it's easier that way. I'll never forget wee Stevie, because I believe when there's the pain of loss to face then, quite naturally, there's part of Stevie in us all. When T.S. Eliot wrote in 'Four Quartets'[13] : 'Humankind cannot bear very much reality', I remember Stevie and I can understand why.

Of course we wish we could protect people from the reality of death and the pain of loss – but we cannot. Of course we wish we could shield people from the torture of the truth that we will all die and we will all face the reality of grief – but we cannot. Of course we wish we could protect generations yet to come from the pain of loss we have experienced in our own day – but we cannot. Are we, then, to do nothing in our helplessness? Or are we to do what we can? What is needed is an understanding from our own perspective, an acceptance of the shock of disbelief in light of our own unwillingness to embrace the pain of loss. And then we can offer this: a willingness to wait for the devastation, the veritable tidal wave of grief which will surely come, and, from our shared experience, to wait again with patience until healing comes.

Notes

10 E,M. Forster (1879–1970), from *Two Cheers for Democracy*, part 2, 'What I believe'. Reproduced with permission of the Provost and Scholars of King's College, Cambridge, and the Society of Authors as the Literary Representatives of the E.M. Forster Estate.

11 Lewis Carroll (1832–1989), *Alice's Adventures in Wonderland*, chapter 5.

12 Anonymous French proverb

13 T.S. Eliot (1888–1965), from 'Burnt Norton' in *Four Quartets*, published by Faber & Faber Ltd.

To know and not to know

To know
and not to know
that you are gone.
To know
I've let you go.
The stone is there,
your name,
your life in chiselled granite
is the truth,
to tell, to know
that you are gone.

And not to know –
a heart cannot believe
what sorrow brings.
While head can know,
can heart accept
and let you go?
I do not know,
and in that moment when I see you there,
and hear your voice,
and smell your sweet perfume,
and know it is not true.
For then I don't believe what words shout loud
that you are gone.

To know
and not to know.
Inhabiting that world
between reality and dreams,
those strange extremities of truth and hope,
of head and heart,
of letting go and holding on,

is to be real,
this is reality for me.

I know
and let you go
and journey ever on
to trudge through missing days.

And not to know,
when missing you brings too much pain,
and wanting you,
and keeping you
brings joy.

To know and not to know.
For it will be forever so.

Too soon to die

They've put a little flower beside your head,
it's red – carnation red –
so deep and strong
against the pillow white.

Your face is turned away,
your eyelids closed.
Did you not like the flower they placed
beside your head?
Was it the fiery red
that made you turn aside?
Would gentle pink have been the better shade?

Yet I think not.
It was no flower that you did shun,
but life itself
in reds and pinks and rainbow hues.
From this you turned away,
and me,
and closed your eyes
to see no more
what flower,
what shade,
what love beside you lies.

They've put a little flower beside your head,
and it will die with you.
And vibrant red will wither soon
to faded brown,
and pinks and rainbow hues will turn to dust.

Too soon,
too soon to die.

So shout, you vibrant red,
and hold my gaze,
and keep me here a while,
to wonder still at beauty here
in you.
Though you see not what I must see,
I feast my eyes
on flower and you.
And even now,
in this eternal time,
see life being lived for you
again
in all its rainbow hues.

What now is real?

What now is real,
when all I knew has crumbled into dust?
    God, make your blessing real once more.

What then is hope,
when all I hoped for will not ever be?
    God, give me hope, to raise me up.

What is my life,
when all of life is threatened by this pain?
    God, let my life be born anew.

What still is love,
when love has gone and left an empty void?
    God, show me love that never dies.

What is the way,
when marker-posts no longer give a sign?
    God, where's the way that I should know?

What now for me,
now light has died and left a future dark?
    God, take my hand now I'm afraid.

What is my God,
what is, what was, what will my God become?
    God, show yourself that I might know.

What now? What next,
When not to know's the hardest place to be?
    God, do you know, and will you say?

Three

Final moments

'O Death, where is thy sting-a-ling-a-ling'
Anon

'To give light to those who sit in the shadow of death'
Bible: Luke 1:79

When I was a small boy I used to go to the cinema in Fort William every Saturday to follow the adventures of my celluloid heroes. Mostly, they were cowboys, for that was the *genre* of the generation. Every good guy wore a white hat. Every bad guy was as ugly as sin. Stereotypes abounded! So it was with the images of death for small boys who knew no better. For in these movie-fantasies-masquerading-as-reality, Indians rolled spectacularly out of the saddle and fell peaceful-faced in the dirt. Men were shot at point-blank range with not a sign of blood or pain – none of the gore and messiness so common in movies now. And after the battle, the hero's side-kick would be cradled in his arms and, smiling, would whisper, 'Tell my maw I love her ...', and breathe his last, usually with violins swelling the music to a not-a-dry-eye-in-the-house type climax. Those were the days – when death was presented with sanitised, neatly-packaged, avoidance-of-reality images for the children – and adults too, I found out later. It's not that I wasn't aware of death. It happens. I wasn't daft. We'd had a budgie that had died. But the images of death in the movies were always carefully stage-managed to make them more palatable and easier to cope with.

I recall one scene – the actual movie is now forgotten in the mists of time – when one of the heroes is shot in an ambush by the bad guys, and lies cradled in the arms of the minister, the preacher-man.

(What a black-suited clergyman was doing in the movie and how he turned up at Lurcher's Gulf in the middle of an ambush, to be at the right place at the right time, I cannot now recall ... I suppose it just fitted the script!) And in the dying moments the minister says something like, 'Don't worry, son. You'll make it, you'll pull through.' And the cowboy croaks. 'Naw, preacher, this is it, the final round-up. I'm off to that great ranch in the sky. But don't worry, I'll save you a place at the chuck-wagon.' And with a smile, he dies. Ah, they don't make them like that any more ...

Now, I'm not sure what this did to my psyche, or how such images have influenced the collective psyche of my generation and others before or since. But I do know that for many people that scene encapsulates the image of what death ought to be, or what they would want it to be. Death should be controlled and beautiful, where everyone is at peace with everyone else and the dying person is at peace with their eternal soul; where final words are said with eloquence, clarity, meaning and significance; where with the dying breath the head rolls gently to the side, and death, just like the dying individual, is cradled in the arms of love and understanding.

Indeed – and I offer this as a little aside, as I'll return to this issue at the end of the chapter – it begins to introduce the idea that death cannot be complete unless the preacher, the minister, the holy-man, the priest, the magical-mystery-man is there to make sense of this dying business. There is often a tension expressed by Roman Catholic families, for example, for the priest to be present at the moment of death to 'do the necessary' so that, in religious or spiritual terms, death is handled in the right and proper way. But, as I've said, more of this later.

Such images of dying, like that played out at Lurcher's Gulf for the benefit of a small boy, may be true in the movies, or indeed may be indelibly stamped on our collective psyche, but they are seldom true in real life. Death brings to those who live with their fantasies the painful reality that the end of life is often very far from pretty. 'O Death, where is thy sting-a-ling-a-ling?'[14] Death can be, and often is, out of control, very ugly, offensive and hellish. The stresses of the dying process often put people at odds with each other and find them vying for centre stage. The end of life brings with it anxieties and restlessness and disturbance. The face of the dying man or woman can often be in torment, and, far from eloquent words being uttered as a comfort to those about to be bereaved, the final moments are often accompanied by a rattling throat and a gasping for breath.

Of course death can be peaceful and dignified and the end can come with completeness and beauty. Thankfully I have seen that often enough and know what a solid platform it can create for those who are bereaved. Indeed, it has been said that one of the principal roles of palliative care and the hospice movement is 'managing dying' so that the end can be as dignified as people would wish and deserve. It is a privilege to be part of that process. But if that is all we expect, then we will remain unprepared for the harsh reality of the other side of death, the messy, unpredictable, horrible side, which is just as possible, just as real, and just as common. Death doesn't come neatly packaged as some old movies would suggest.

Let me offer an insight from another facet of life. Some years into our marriage, my wife and I shared a kind of 'marriage encounter' process with two good friends, David and Barbara. It was a very simple set-up – and, ultimately, very helpful for all of us. It took the form of both couples meeting weekly for four weeks over lunch, and, on each occasion, one of us taking a turn to share our thoughts about marriage and be supported in our explorations by the experience, insights and honesty of the other three. The first three weeks had gone well. We all felt good about what we were sharing together, and Mary and I felt very supported and nurtured in our own relationship. It was my turn on week four. I'd prepared well for my opportunity, and, when the time came, I had in my hand a little piece of paper on which I'd jotted my thoughts. I had three points to make, and each had three sub-sections. When I'd gone through 1a to 3c very carefully, I paused to await the discussion. I was not prepared for what happened next. David leaned across the table. 'Nothing's as tidy as that,' he said. 'It's way too neat! Maybe telling the truth, with all its ragged edges, might be better.' It was as if he'd taken my carefully scripted piece of paper, torn it into little pieces, and thrown them up in the air. I was furious! What right had this man to challenge my neat and tidy world?

Looking back, my anger has dissipated and I now remember that moment as the beginning of the dawning of an important truth. We talked about it then and I've thought about it often since. Of necessity, and most of the time, life is full of rough edges. We have to live with messiness and untidy, unfinished parts of our lives. It's never as neat as we would want it to be, or, indeed, as we would want others to believe it to be. It doesn't fall into neatly scripted categories or areas like my 1a to 3c. We learn to live with the rough edges and not believe that everything can be tied up with red ribbon all of the time, in marriage or anything else. My neat and tidy world, or at least my expression of it, was the better for being challenged.

The reality of death is no different. For us to believe that death can be scripted or stage-managed, like a childhood movie-memory or a tidy explanation of the meaning of marriage, is living in fantasy and believing it is reality. Death, like life, cannot and should not be tied up with red ribbon. It does not come neatly packaged. It has to be faced with all its rough edges, unfinished business, ugliness and pain. That is what is real.

The tensions between the tidy image and the messy reality are, however, very common and take many forms. Take, for example, the pressure people put themselves under, or are put under by others, to be present at the final moment when the candle of life burns its last. Such a desire to be there at the end is created and reinforced by many things. It arises out of a desire to 'do it right', and, in the minds of many people, that means that loyalty to the dying person is expressed in the faithfulness of the bedside vigil and the assurance that you have stuck it out to the end. 'I didn't let her down' is the way such a decision is expressed when things work out to the satisfaction of the devoted carer. This pressure to be there at the end is often created out of a promise made to the dying person, the committed 'yes' to the question, 'You'll never leave me, will you? I don't want to die alone.' It carries with it the unspoken belief that if such a promise is broken then some 'punishment', and certainly bucket-loads of guilt, will ensue. And it is also born out of a fascination with the moment of death itself. For many of those who take the role of the faithful companion on the road to death have no experience of death and the dying process. They are drawn, therefore, with a kind of morbid curiosity to that ultimate moment of the expiry of life. Whatever the reason, having committed themselves 'to be there at the death', the pressure to see it through is enormous. And, sadly, for many who make that commitment, the reality does not work out the way it was planned.

Take Edith, for example. Edith was an only daughter, unmarried and devoted to her mother. In her mid-sixties and still fit and active, she was her mother's carer, and an excellent job she had made of it too. When her mother was dying, Edith kept her at home for as long as she was able, and then, with her mother's full agreement, saw her settled into the hospice for the final stage of her journey of life. Her mother knew she was dying, and Edith knew so too. And, a few days before she died, she promised her mother that she wouldn't leave her, that she would stay with her right to the end.

And so it was that, when it was clear to the medical and nursing staff that the end was near, Edith began her bedside vigil. She stayed overnight in her mother's room, a devoted daughter at a mother's bedside. She strove to stay awake beside her now unconscious mother, giving her the tender loving care she had promised. The following night, she did the same, as her mother lingered on. The trouble with death, however, is that it does not fit neatly into pigeon-holes of time or style. Nor is there any pre-prepared script. Of course it was obvious that Edith's mother was close to the end. But the reality was that the end was taking a bit longer to come around than anyone could have predicted. And, in the process, Edith was wearing herself out. On the third day, she decided to go home for a shower and a rest. Her mother's condition was stable. There had been no real change for nearly twenty-four hours. It was time to take the chance of absenting herself from the bedside. Edith arrived home as the phone was ringing. It was the hospice to tell her that her mother had died.

Now, who knows … ? Did Edith's mother need her not to be there in order to let go of life? Did a dying person need to be freed from the vigil of those around her in order to slip quietly away? Is there something in the subconscious of the dying person that wishes to protect their loved ones from the pain of the final moment of death? Did death need to happen in silence and alone-ness and not in the presence of watchers and waiters? We'll never know, because Edith's mother will not come back to tell us. But two things I do know … The first is that more people die like Edith's mother when the family have gone away than would appear to be random chance. There are many theories as to why this might be. But all I know is that it is extremely common. And the second thing I know is that Edith – as with many a devoted carer before her and since – was distraught at the news of her mother's death. She had, as she saw it, failed her mother. She had let her down. She had broken her promise. And she was broken-hearted as a result.

We know that we cannot predict the moment of death. And we know that Edith's faithfulness was above and beyond the call. And we know that no one had done anything wrong at any stage of this dying journey. But was any of that a comfort to Edith? No chance!

I recall working with Walter some months after his wife had died. He told me he was still haunted by the moment of her dying. Sitting by her bedside as he had promised, and struggling to stay awake in the wee small hours, he fell asleep – for a few seconds or a few minutes, he never knew – and when he woke up his wife was dead. The image of his dead wife and the failure of not being really 'with her' at the end was all-consuming. The guilt of letting her down was a crippling burden in bereavement. It took months of careful work with Walter, as with Edith, to get things into perspective, to help him see that it was the whole of his faithfulness that mattered, and that a few seconds of sleep at the end could never destroy that. But, as with Edith, it was hard for Walter because of the commitment he had made. And even now, many years on from his wife's death, he tells me that his moment of what he describes as failure is still a big factor in his life.

I have come to realise that these moments of Edith's and Walter's 'failure', and the guilt they cause and the burdens they create for the bereavement journey, are very real and should not be dismissed. So I use the image of a photo-album with such people, and for many it is a helpful way of dealing with this issue. The photo-album which contains all the memories and images of the person you have loved has many pages. But for a while after a death, all that seems to happen is that it falls open at the 'death page', and the image of death, the horror of the dying, or the guilt at your 'failure' is the page and the memory which predominates. That's the way it is and the way it has to be. You cannot tear that page from the album, and you cannot stop the album from opening there. What's done is done. What's there is there.

In time, however, you will turn to other pages, dwell on other images and relive other memories. Sometimes you will do that on purpose, to force yourself away from the images of death, to try to balance them with happier days. Sometimes it will happen spontaneously, when something will remind you of a moment, a place, an event which is about living and fullness of life. These other pages may make you sad, or they may make you smile. But you are simply reminding yourself, or being reminded by your memories, that they are there, that the album has many other pages. But, goodness me, does the album not still fall open naturally at the dying page, even when you don't want it to, or even when you have become aware of the other pages there are to look at? So, let it happen. Don't fight it. See that page for what it is, an important page, a recent page, a predominant page, But also see it as one page among many, many more. In time, that is what it will be – one image among many. You will go back to it, and curse it, and relive the pain of its memory, and occasionally you may be drawn to it when you simply don't want to be – the album may fall open at that page for years as it did with Walter. But now you have also come to realise that it is what it is: only one page of a big and important album.

There are ways of helping people accept and come to live with their sense of failure if they have not fulfilled their promise to be there at the end. But perhaps, being aware of the huge burdens it creates for people in their bereavement, we should not choose to put all our eggs in this one 'I must be there at the end' basket, for it is fraught with problems, filled with the probability of disaster, and is a recipe for masses of resulting guilt. Instead, let's recognise that death can never be neatly packaged according to our wishes or hopes, no matter how sincere these are or how committed we are to getting it right.

Another area of tension around the reality of death lies in the field of relationships. Brendan was a forty-five-year-old husband and father. He was a patient in the hospice on a number of occasions during a long and difficult disease process. He had a devoted wife, two grown-up, mature and supportive daughters, and a saintly mother. There was not one person I spent time with in this family circle that I did not like and whom I did not admire in their devotion to Brendan. But there were tensions too. Brendan's wife, Nina, had a very responsible job. And while her company were very supportive and understanding, out of loyalty to her employers and colleagues, and given the protracted nature of Brendan's illness, she was trying to hold down her job and keep that aspect of her life, as well as her home life, stable and organised while still playing her part in the care and visiting of her husband.

Brendan's mother, widowed and free to be away from home, came over from Fife each day – a 50-miles-or-so car journey – and spent time with her son. She was there when Nina came in to the hospice at the end of a day's work. She was there when the visiting time came to an end. She was there when Nina took Brendan out for an afternoon car run, and so she came too. She was there when Nina and Brendan went home for an evening, and she came too. Eventually, it was decided that she should move in to stay with Nina. A sensible and right decision in which everyone was involved. But the tensions just got worse.

The trouble was that they were all such nice people, and even if they were tearing their hair out in private, there was no public squabbling. It's not always like that. In the worst of scenarios we have to cope with openly warring family factions, on occasion with some foul and abusive language exchanged. You see the worst and the best of human nature and family life around the events of a death. But, being so nice, Nina – and it was her I personally dealt with the most through it all – did not know what to do with the tension. She knew Brendan's mother was losing her only son, and it was right that she was there. But she also knew that she was losing her husband, and that she needed time to come to terms with that and time with Brendan to work things through as best they could.

So both these legitimate roles, being worked through by two caring people with the same dying person, created a tension between them as mother and wife competed for centre stage. Did either of them know they were competing? Probably not, and if they did they never admitted it. Did either of them see the competitive edge to their caring? Not that I saw, though they may have had their own private thoughts on the matter. Were either of them bad or insensitive people? Certainly not. Were either of them wrong? I don't believe so. I cannot now recall how the tensions were resolved. I suspect that there were family discussions, when things could be looked at and talked through in an open and honest way. I do know that, together and alone, all members of the family had time to say their goodbyes to Brendan before he died. And I am glad of that.

The other side of this coin is also common. Sadly, I have seen the strains between family members remain unresolved and ultimately become destructive. There is something in a mother, for example, which creates in her the sense that she has to remain protective, and ultimately be the main carer and protector of a dying son, no matter what age he might be or how long or how happily he may have been married. Such is the nature of things, and such are the factors we have to understand. Family tensions are not to be dismissed in the face of death, for we do not live in perfect harmony with one another all of the time. In most of the families I have ever known there are local rules and conventions. Over time, idiosyncrasies come to be accommodated, past histories are absorbed, and quirky behaviour is put to one side for the greater good. We learn to get by and to live in reasonable harmony with one another. But when a trauma comes along to knock the equilibrium of a family's life, such as a death of a main family member, then local rules are often broken, and old wounds are opened.

Is it not understandable, therefore, that a mother losing a son will be in competition with a daughter-in-law losing her husband? And is it any wonder that either might feel that their loss is greater than the other's as they grieve for the death of the same person? Such tensions are the reality. They happen naturally. They are not bad or unwholesome. They don't only arise among nasty people. Brendan's family showed me that. If, then, such tensions can be faced, acknowledged and, indeed, worked through in a respectful way, then the loss for everyone can be understood for what it is: deep and painful, and not something which needs to be compared with other people's experiences and found to be better or worse.

When Victor was dying I slipped into his room to see him, to find two women by his bedside. One introduced herself to me as Victor's wife, the other as his daughter. In conversation I discovered that this was Victor's second wife, his first wife having died many years before, and that the daughter was a child of this marriage. I also discovered that he had two daughters from his first marriage, and that his present wife also had three daughters from her first marriage. Over the next few days I met most of these women, and their partners, and their families. And while these complexities of family trees are not unusual, what sticks in my mind about Victor's family was how respectful each person or group was to the grief of the others. For some it was losing a stepfather, for others it was supporting a mother in her loss. For some it was losing a father, for others it was understanding that a half-sister was also losing her dad. This wasn't a family where everyone got on or even liked each other, I suspect. But this was a family where the people within it, aware of their own needs and losses and the needs and losses of others, worked together for the greater good. And, it seemed to me, here was a family whose capacity to deal with these things offered the right environment to Victor and allowed him to die in peace. Here was a family which had learned 'to give light to those who sit in the shadow of death'[15].

In the end, and at the end, facing the death of a loved one is intensely private. Who really knows your thoughts, your longings, your regrets and your pleasures? With whom do you share not just what you ought to share or are allowed to share, but all you feel and are? So you stay in your private world of loss, in the moment and over time. Sometimes you can make sense of what you experience, and sometimes it will make no sense at all. If, therefore, we know that to be true for ourselves, can we not respectfully understand the grief of others, their privacy and their outbursts, their needs and their losses? Perhaps we should begin from where we are, and, accepting that, begin to understand where others might be in their bereavement journey.

In his moving poem 'On a dead child'[16], the poet Robert Bridges offers these contrasting stanzas:

> *Thy mother's treasure wert thou; – alas! No longer*
> *To visit her heart with wondrous joy; to be*
> *Thy father's pride; ah, he*
> *Must gather his faith together, and his strength make stronger.*

> *So quiet! Doth change content thee? – Death, whither hath he taken thee?*
> *To a world, do I think, that rights the disaster of this?*
> *The vision of which I miss,*
> *Who weep for the body, and wish to warm thee and awaken thee?*

> *Ah! little at best can all our hopes avail us*
> *To lift this sorrow, or sheer us, when in the dark,*
> *Unwilling, alone we embark,*
> *And all the things we have seen and have known and have heard of, fail us.*

So a father recognises that a mother, too, will grieve, and with tender words accepts that this tragic loss has deprived a loving mother of 'her wondrous joy'. And yet, as his thoughts unfold, he returns to the devastation of his own loss, 'thy father's pride', as he struggles to 'gather his faith together' and be strong enough to face the future without his child, with no righting of 'the disaster of this', failed by all the things he had ever seen or known or heard before. Such is the offence of a death and the inevitable selfishness of grief. And such is the need, therefore, to understand the selfishness of others' grief and to respect their grieving out of our own. How hard that is! How lacking in selflessness does the horror of death make us as we seek to handle these final moments aright.

I close this chapter with a 'final moments' story which has left me with a feeling of wonder and mystery. I don't understand it all and, though I've recounted the story many times, I've stopped analysing it. I simply know that what happened was right and good.

We had a family in our hospice as their mum was dying who could only be described as 'harum-scarum' – too many people, too much anguish, too many mobile phones, too much hassle. When the old lady died, I was surprised to be approached by one of the nurses with the information that the family were asking for 'The Last Rites' for mum. I was surprised – because not only were they not Roman Catholic, they'd never been part of any faith community or church; because I hadn't been involved before; and because their mother had already died. But this isn't too unusual a situation, for, as I've suggested at the start of this chapter, people often have a kind of concept, a picture about what you do when someone dies, when 'the holy man' has to come and 'do the necessary', to do what's right, to round it all off properly. This time the 'holy man' was me, and the call was for someone to help make sense of the final moments.

I was tired. It was the end of what had been a very stressful day. I could have well done without this. It was one more thing too much to respond to. But, needs must ... So, a weary carer, I went along to the room, and, in the midst of the distress of a large crowd of people – 'Oh, thanks for coming, son, you'll know what to do' – I read the 23rd Psalm, 'The Lord is my shepherd ...', said a short prayer, offered a blessing, and gave a commendation with a hand laid on the brow of their mother. Then, I took my leave – too rapidly, perhaps, but hoping that I hadn't communicated any of my unwillingness to stay – leaving the little Bible from which I'd read the Psalm on the cover of the bed as a gift to help them remember the occasion. Whatever had been done, the family appeared to be very grateful.

I expected no more contact with the family. What was done was done. I just wanted to get home. As I was tidying up my office ready to leave at the end of the day, the phone rang. 'Tom,' the receptionist said, 'there's a Sharon on the phone. She says she knows you.' 'OK, put her through.' 'Hello,' the voice said. 'It's Sharon. Jessie's daughter. I was in the room earlier on when you did yon thing for ma Mammy.' 'Oh yes, Sharon, I remember. How are you all?' 'Oh, not too bad now,' she replied. 'But …' She paused. 'But … see yon Bible you left.' 'Uh, huh,' I responded. 'Well, ma sister took it away.' 'That's OK, Sharon,' I protested. 'It was there for someone to use. It was OK for her to take it.' 'Well,' she continued – and there was another pause – 'have you got any more? See, ah want one. And there's my ither sister. An' ma lassie. An' ma two nieces …' I was gobsmacked. 'How many would you like?' I asked. 'Ah'll take six …' came the reply. So six Bibles were put in a large envelope to be picked up from the receptionist that evening. And, indeed, the six Bibles were duly collected later for appropriate distribution by the bold Sharon.

That night I went home from work with all my tiredness gone. I had cared. Of course I had. Companionship and compassion had been offered in large measure. And now I needed my space, my rest, the love of my wife, my relaxation, my prayer, my God, my telly, my crossword, my dram … I knew how important it is for carers to care for themselves. But on this night there was another dimension. On this occasion – and I still don't really understand why – the final moments had made some sense to a grieving family – and, once again, for me.

The final moments of death will cause us to react as we react. Whether it is the cocoon of shock or the lashing out at bad news, the failure at not getting it right or dealing with family tensions, we may never be completely prepared for the moment of death. We may never be ready for our own reactions or the reactions of others. But if we can be aware of that, and understand the messy reality rather than the sanitised, movie-fantasy of death, then we can become more accepting of ourselves, more patient with others, more tolerant of our differences, and even more amazed at those moments of wonder and peace.

Notes

14 Anonymous, from a popular song in the British Army in the 1914–18 War, 'O Death, where is thy sting-a-ling-a-ling, O Grave, thy victoree? The bells of Hell go ting-a-ling-a-ling for you but not for me.'

15 Luke 1:79

16 Robert Bridges (1844–1930), from 'On a dead child', quoted with thanks from www.cnglishverse.com

The moment

I waited for the moment
when she would breathe her last.
I held my own breath
in the gaps in her breathing.
I wondered, with childish expectation,
about the moment of her dying.
And I was transfixed
by my waiting and my unknowing.

In that dying moment
when a shallow breath was followed by no other,
Like an ebbing tide
that ceased to throw a gentle wave upon the shore,
In that thankful release
of my own breath held for an eternity,
That drew no more response
from this, her lifeless frame,
In that awesome wonder
and utter fascination
Of this precious moment
of the extinction of life itself,
I was transfixed.

But now,
when waiting was no more,
My scant knowing was, for now, completed here
by this moment of the mystery of death.

I had waited for the moment,
and in its coming
and now its going
I was complete
for now,
As the moment had
transformed my life.

I have often thought about my own death. What would it be like? How would I handle it? What would I say? What would I do? The answers to these questions are, 'I don't know', for while I can fantasise and wonder, I will never know till I am there. But I have hopes, and I have ideas, and I have pictures in my mind which I hope I will be able to draw upon when the time comes. And, if I'm not able to make sense of it, and maybe even get it wrong, then I'll leave this reflection for you to ponder, the kind of things I'd like to be able to say, especially to my children.

Today

Today I give you this light,
lit from the lamps of those who've shown me the way,
nurtured when it burned low,
held high when it shone so bright –
and now I let it go into your hands.
Today, I give you my light.

Today I give you this word,
learned from the wisdom of those who've searched out their truth,
tested and made my own,
added to from the little I've learned –
and here, I trust you with this word for your truth.
Today, I give you my word.

Today I give you this faith,
formed from the faith of those who've moulded my belief.
I've formed it and reformed it,
now misshapen, now a thing of wonder –
and see, I let it go for you, to speak of what you need to know.
Today, I give you my faith.

Today I give you this love,
uniquely my love, yet nurtured by loving I've known,

drawn from the pool of eternal love,
and practised in time –
and look, because I believe you will use well this gift,
today, I give you my love.

Today I give you these dreams,
borrowed from dreamers and nurtured with my own hope,
what has sustained me
and what has cast me down –
so go, learn from your hopes and be shaped by your own possibilities.
Today, I give you my dreams.

Today I give you this life,
what you will speak of and what you will never discover.
Here is my living,
not threatened by dying.
Here, look, now, I let it go, no longer mine, to make of what you will.
Today, I give you this, my life.

A prayer at the bedside of a dying patient

God of the moment –
I have no words to offer now,
no prayers to say that will be right.
So, fill this moment with your present Grace.
God of the moment, make this moment yours.

God, the companion –
I do so little now
that makes me feel I'm doing any good at all.
So, be for me the friend I need to know as time unfolds.
God, the Companion, make my purpose yours.

God of our healing –
I understand so little of your healing touch,
and know that death will come to challenge Love itself.
So, come and gather up this pain and loss, and hold it close.
God, with your healing, make this dying yours.

God of our emptiness –
I feel so lonely here, devoid of strength and hope,
and wonder even now where faith has gone.
So, make your promise true, again, for me, for now.
God, fill my emptiness with a presence that's yours.

God of our sorrow –
I know you cried our tears when Christ had lost a friend,
and need you now to weep with me.
So weep, and with our mingled tears let me be one with you.
God of my sorrow, make this sorrow yours.

God of uncertain days –
I do not know what life will hold or what I'll do,
and realise that life begins again right here, right now, for me.
So, in the mystery of my unknowing, come and be real again.
God of the unknown, make my journey yours.

Four

Promises made, promises broken

'For I have promises to keep
And miles to go before I sleep'
Robert Frost: 'Stopping by Woods on a Snowy Evening'

'Who broke no promise, serv'd no private end,
Who gain'd no title, and who lost no friend.'
Alexander Pope: 'To Mr Addison'

Promises made in the process of dying and around the events of a death can be either crippling burdens to carry or pleasures to explore. When such a promise, and loyalty to the person to whom it was made, unhelpfully constrains those who are bereaved – or more likely one bereaved individual – it becomes an entrapment. But when it is a task that can be fulfilled, enabling those who fulfil it – again, more than likely one bereaved person – to enhance the relationship and their commitment to the person who has died, then it can be a liberation.

When Roddy was dying at home, he and his wife Megan had lots of time to talk. Roddy was thirty-five and he and Megan had been married for six or seven years. They had a little boy, Anthony, who had just turned five. Roddy was deteriorating rapidly with an aggressive cancer, having only been diagnosed a few months before. It was hard to talk and plan ahead. Doing that made them face the reality of Roddy's death, and that was a bitter-sweet thing. They were trying to be sensible and organised and open, but every time they got into 'that stuff', as Roddy called it, it was about facing death, and it all seemed too hopeless. But on their own, and together with myself and others, they talked, and their sharing was important.

I was with the family shortly after Roddy died. The house was full of tensions and anger. Megan hadn't slept and was finding it hard to think straight. Roddy's parents had come down from the north of Scotland and were adding to the tension. A mother who had lost her son was distraught. A father went into organising mode and was, to put it simply, trying to organise too many things, for too many people, with too little consultation, in too short a time. Megan asked if she could have a private word with me. We sat in the loo, the only quiet place in the house at that time. And with Megan perched on the toilet seat and me sitting on the edge of the bath, she told me a little of what she and Roddy had talked about. Some of it was around his wishes for his funeral. Most of that was pretty straightforward stuff about readings, and hymns, and pieces of music, and the like. But the bit that was distressing Megan the most was the promise made to Roddy about the scattering of his ashes. He wanted to be cremated and have his ashes scattered in St Bride's Bay, near St David's Head in south-west Wales, where Megan's family originated from, where she and Roddy had met, and where, with Anthony, they had spent many happy holidays. He knew that his parents would not wish this at all. He was sure they would want him buried in the family graveyard in the north of Scotland, 'back home' as they saw it. So he had made Megan promise that his ashes would be scattered in Wales. And she had. And that was fine – except she now had to deliver on the promise.

She knew it was going to be difficult. She had a picture in her mind of being with Anthony and scattering the ashes together, privately, intimately, creating a bond and a memory that would sustain them in their journey of grief. But she also had a reality to face, of opposition, of pressure, of a lack of understanding, of being forced, perhaps, to break a promise. And what would Roddy think of her if she did that? And how would she live with a promise made and a promise broken? A promise made in love, a promise to keep, and, with Robert Frost[17], 'miles to go before I sleep' in the worry of fulfilling it. All this was creating in Megan an unbearable tension.

It was good that Megan and Roddy had talked together, and it was really good that they had come to a decision that Roddy was happy with and which would be helpful to Megan and Anthony. The fulfilling of the promise was, however, a different matter. As it turned out, Megan was right. Roddy's parents were upset, and Megan had to be clear about why the promise had been made, her wish to be loyal to Roddy's desires and the importance to her of keeping her promise. I knew all of this, because I'd been asked to come next day to talk it all through – or to referee, as I put it later – as the funeral was being planned. And, as is often the case, a compromise was reached. Whether everyone was happy with the compromise I'll never know, but at least they were able to give a little ground and see the other point of view. Would they have been able to work it out together if I hadn't been there? Well, maybe not so well. But at least we came up with decisions that were workable and allowed Megan's promise to be kept. Roddy was indeed cremated. Most of his ashes were scattered on his favourite beach, and Megan told me later it was a very special moment for her and Anthony. A portion of the ashes were taken up to the north of Scotland and were interred in the family graveyard with appropriate Presbyterian dignity. A stone was raised in the old churchyard with Roddy's name on it, alongside that of his uncles and grandmother.

Megan and Anthony moved down to Wales a year or so later. I don't know what has happened to them as we've not kept in touch. But I hope that a little boy runs along a beach and remembers his dad. And I hope a grieving widow still sheds tears of loss and of joy as she feels close to her husband.

But what if a promise had been made and agreed to that was unworkable? What if Roddy had insisted he be interred in the penalty box at Hampden Park so that he could be close to the action when

Scotland eventually scored a goal? And what if Megan had agreed, simply to give a dying man comfort and solace, with no intention of following through on a promise made? And what if she'd sorted that out in her head, until she realised that she'd made a promise and now couldn't fulfil it when Roddy had died? And what if she was then in turmoil because she was letting him down, and heaped with guilt because she'd broken a promise, and even – and I've heard this said too – frightened that Roddy's soul wouldn't be at peace, or would even come back to disturb her, because he wasn't laid to rest when and how he had wished? What if ... Such promises create an entrapment which messes up the grief process. 'Who broke no promise ...'[18] We get a glimpse of that with Megan, but, in her case, we also see the rightness of the promise and find a methodology to work it through. But if the promise is unworkable, and is simply made out of loyalty or even to 'get someone off your back', what then?

'You'll hae a pipe-band at the funeral,' Charlie insisted, 'and the mourners are no' to wear black. You're a' to wear bright colours. And, I won't be able to stand it if the undertaker wears yon tail-coat and strippit troosers. So get them to wear bright shirts and flowery ties. And you're no' to wear yon dog-collar and be straight-laced. Hae a laugh, man, and dinnae mak' them greet. For I'll be a lang time deid!' I laughed when Charlie told me that. I laughed with him at the image he'd put in my mind of the dour, pasty-faced funeral director and his staff dressed in yellow shirts and floral ties. I shared that with the local undertaker later on. He didn't see the joke.

So Charlie's wishes were unworkable, and I never made the promise. But what I did do was to talk with him about what was workable and what wasn't, and what the 'feel' of the funeral would be, guided by his ideas but not entrapped by the detail. And that, it seemed to me, was the right approach. For to make promises that are unworkable, while placating the dying person and making them feel their wishes are being taken seriously and at the same time creating a tyranny for those that are left, is singularly unhelpful and a potential barrier to a positive grief process.

It's the possibility, or the necessity, that the promise may have to be broken that causes the problems. There are two ways of dealing with this. The first is to have a laugh with Charlie. In openness you can make it clear to him that you are taking him seriously, that you know what he means and that you'll take that on board. But you can also know and say that a funeral and the aftermath of it is for those who are left, and what's planned and delivered has to be workable in the circumstances in which those who are bereaved find themselves. So, one way of dealing with the potential problems is not to be trapped by promises by not making them in the first place.

The second way is to make the promise, within reason, in sincerity and love, to indicate that you will try to fulfil it according to the wishes expressed, or simply to say yes, that's fine, and to know in the making of the promise that it will almost certainly be broken. There will be no restlessness of the spirit of the dead person if a promise remains unfulfilled. There need be no guilt.

Rita was an elderly widow we had in our hospice who was dying slowly from her cancer, but we were more concerned about her rapidly increasing dementia. She was a delightful woman, a devout Christian, and no bother at all to care for – apart from the fact that she wandered around a bit and forgot where her room was from time to time. One day the doctor had to explain to Rita that she wasn't going to have any more chemotherapy because it was no longer doing her any good. She was seriously ill and chemotherapy wasn't going to help. In fact, it would probably make her worse. Rita asked him if she was dying. The doctor said she was – not imminently, but it was clear her cancer was progressing and there was never going to be a cure. It was as if Rita was hearing this for the first time. Of course, she had been told before. She had even explored it with me some weeks previously. But, because of her dementia, either she hadn't taken it in

or she'd simply forgotten. So, for Rita, 'bad news' was being broken
for the first time. It was devastating. She was distraught.

I was asked to spend time with her later in the morning. I was
always pleased to spend time with Rita, and we talked through what
she'd been told and how distressed and frightened she was. She held
my hand – in what, with her bony fingers and wasted arms, was a
close approximation of a vice-like grip – and gazed at me with plead-
ing eyes. 'I'll not be left alone?' she asked. 'No, there'll always be
someone with you,' I replied. 'They'll keep giving me my tablets?'
she asked. 'Yes, they'll still do that and keep caring for you in all your
needs,' I answered. 'Promise me you'll come to my funeral,' she said.
And I paused. Of course I could promise that she would have
companionship and good care in her dying. But now I was being
asked to promise something I did not know I could fulfil. It wasn't a
difficult promise. It wasn't as if she was asking to be buried on the top
of Kilimanjaro or requesting that the Dagenham Girl Pipers come to
play at her bedside. It was a simple promise, simply asked. It was a
request for reassurance, for security, for peace of mind.

But what was I to say? I knew full well that I might not be able to
deliver on this promise. I could be on holiday, busy with something
else I couldn't get out of, languishing on a sick-bed, or whatever. I
did not know the day or the time of her funeral, so I did not know
whether I could fulfil the promise. And, of course, I could have told
her that. I could have said, 'Yes, if I can, but it might not be possible,
so I'll do my best …' But I didn't. I looked her in the eye, and I said,
'Yes, Rita, I'll be there.' And she smiled.

Some weeks later Rita left the hospice to go to the South of
England to live with her sister. I don't know what happened to her.
So I don't know whether I will need to keep the promise I've made
to her, or whether, if Rita has died, I was never called upon to make
that decision one way or another. But I will not be burdened with
guilt. I will keep my promise if I can. And if I can't, then I can't. But

the value of my promise to Rita was in the making of the promise, in that moment of pastoral care, of sensitivity, of weighing up the pros and cons in that instant of being put on the spot and seeing that her 'peace of mind' was the predominating issue. A promise had been made. And a promise may be broken. But love had been shared and peace of mind had been offered, and that has to be right.

There are other kinds of promise made around the dying process which can cause anxiety for those who are bereaved. Promises are not just about wishes for a funeral and whether they can be carried through or not. There are the promises centred on the place of care and ultimately of death, and there are the promises around what people will or will not do with their lives after their loved one has gone. I have a chapter in *A Need for Living* which is entitled 'Pilot in home waters' which tells the story of a distraught daughter who felt she had failed her mother by agreeing that she come into the hospice to die. She had promised – and her mother had made her promise – that her mother would die in her own bed and that she would care for her at home right to the end. But the end was hellish, and now that the caring was beyond her ability it had to be the hospice for the good of all. But because a promise had been made and was being broken, there was a huge burden of failure already placed on a caring daughter's shoulders. I used the image with her of the hospice staff being the pilot coming onto the bridge of a great ship to guide it gently into the home port. She was still in charge. She hadn't failed. She had taken the ship through very stormy waters. And we were just there to help bring the ship home safely. That helped a bit, and she knew in her head that she had done the right thing and that the image made sense. But in her heart she knew the promise she had made, and now that her mother was beyond talking with, there was no way the promise could be altered and the current circumstances used to ease the burden of guilt already created. I don't know what happened to that daughter in her loss. I hope my image helped. But

I suspect that her promise created a tension in bereavement between head and heart, and, I would reckon, the journey of loss might have had a difficult beginning.

If you make that kind of promise, often for all the good reasons that lay behind my promise to Rita – pastoral responsibility, peace of mind, easing of anxieties, and the like – then you have to make it with the full knowledge that you might not be able to fulfil it. If you can't fulfil it, then you have to know that you haven't failed; you must not beat yourself up by believing that the promise shouldn't have been made in the first place. Perhaps we would do well to project ourselves a little into the world of what it might be like when we are dying, and make a decision now not to put intolerable pressure on our loved ones to agree to promises which will entrap them in the future and make bereavement worse for them than it need be. Can we do that? I hope we can, so that we offer a caring rather than a destructive environment for those who are left behind.

There is a final area of this promise business that is important, and that is around promises which are made to dying people about how those who are left will, or will not, live their lives. When I was a parish minister, I knew a delightful elderly couple, Wally and Chrissie, who lived in the bottom half of a huge Victorian villa in a very smart part of Edinburgh. When Wally died and Chrissie was left alone, she rattled about this big house like a dried pea in a box. It had been too big for both of them, and now it was way too big for her on her own. In time it became an increasing struggle for Chrissie to manage. The issue of moving to a sheltered-housing complex or even a nursing home had to be looked at. And it fell to me to be one of those who explored the subject with her.

Chrissie was an intelligent woman and still articulate even in her frailty She understood perfectly the reasons why she should move. But, in the middle of our discussion, she started to cry. And through her sobs she said, 'But I promised Wally I would never leave here.

We had sixty-two years together in this house. There are so many memories, I would feel I was abandoning him if I moved away. I made him a promise, and I have to keep that promise now. I'll never be able to forgive myself if I break my promise to Wally.'

I could understand that, as I suspect you can too. The common sense thing would have been to sell up and move out – and, actually, seeing Chrissie in the state she was in, I believe Wally would have understood that too. But common sense wasn't the issue here. The heart ruled the head. She had made a promise, and she couldn't break it.

In time, the situation resolved itself in a tragic but strangely complete way. Chrissie fell and fractured her hip – 'I got the leg of the Zimmer tangled with the table leg and my own leg tangled with them both, and I didn't know which leg to move first, so I fell over ...,' Chrissie told me with a smile when I went to visit her in hospital. And, you see, hospital was OK, because she'd fallen and, therefore, had to be there. She hadn't moved out of the house by choice. Chrissie never got out of hospital. She developed pneumonia and died peacefully. A few days before she died – and she had decided not to take antibiotics but to let nature take its course – this weak and frail lady held my hand and whispered, 'I kept my promise, didn't I?' And she had, and she died at peace as a result. Did she know she was dying? Of course she did. Was she letting go because to have returned to the house would have been to wrestle with the promise once again? Oh, I very much suspect so.

So promises made can be a tyranny, an entrapment, about the way people live in bereavement and the options which may be closed off to them in the unfolding of the new phase of their lives. My wife and I had a discussion recently about what we were likely to do if one of us were to die, especially if it were to happen before we were really old – and, no, we don't talk about death and dying all the time; it just happened to come up. I told Mary that she shouldn't feel trapped by a loyalty to me and that if someone else was to come along she shouldn't feel inhibited from exploring a new relationship. She suggested that she couldn't even contemplate wanting another relationship, and that she would likely as not be happy on her own. But, none the less, she appreciated the point that was being made.

But if I – or she, indeed – had said something like, 'When I go, you are not to look at another relationship. No way! What would the children think? And why would you need to anyway?', what kind of entrapment would that have created in loss as a new journey of life was unfolding? And what turmoil there would be if one of us were to fall in love again – even if we cannot contemplate that happening – when we had made a promise or felt under pressure not to do so?

I began this chapter by suggesting that promises made in the process of dying and around the events of a death can be either crippling burdens to carry or options to explore. When promises set boundaries that constrain people in their grief, then they are unhelpful. But when they are tasks to fulfil, and they offer a sense of purpose to the journey of bereavement, then that can indeed be a liberation. Mary Lee Hall[19], in the words read at the funeral of Diana, Princess of Wales, by Diana's sister, offers us this insight:

If I should die and leave you here a while,
Be not like others, sore undone, who keep
Long vigil by the silent dust and weep.
For my sake turn again to life and smile,
Nerving thy heart and trembling hand to do
That which will comfort other souls than thine;
Complete these unfinished tasks of mine,
And I, perchance, may therein comfort you.

So let Lawrence have the final word about promises. His story tells you of the completion of an unfinished task and the comfort it brought to him in his loss.

Lawrence and his wife Marjorie had been lifelong companions. They had known each other in school, and, after a few years' separation during the War, had been married in 1946. I got to know them both when they were in their 40s. They were a lovely couple and I came to like them very much indeed. Lawrence and Marjorie had no children, much to their regret, but they both had elderly parents to whom they were devoted. They were teachers, and, over the years, had progressed within their profession, Lawrence into management and Marjorie within her chosen subject. They were a model of a happy couple.

Lawrence and Marjorie had a dream that one day, perhaps in retirement or perhaps sooner, they would have the holiday of a lifetime in the Grand Canyon in the USA, a place they had always loved. But it never seemed to happen. Work commitments, then the illness of one parent or another, always seemed to get in the way. There was no stress in that, just the putting off of their dream for now, the shelving of an idea until its time was right. Over the years Lawrence and Marjorie nursed their elderly parents through different illnesses, and, in the space of a few years, had to cope with the death of all four of them, a series of deaths which, though tragic, they managed with remarkable fortitude.

Retirement wasn't far away, and, given a good pension provision and money left by parents, they decided to cut loose from work a couple of years early. Now was the time to work on their dream, and plans for the trip to the Grand Canyon were laid. Sadly, they never got to share their dream. Marjorie took a stroke soon after retirement, and, following a period of typically devoted attention from Lawrence, slipped quietly from life.

Naturally, Lawrence was devastated and, to be quite frank, had an immense struggle to pull himself together as the bereavement journey unfolded. He had lost all purpose, and found it very hard to motivate himself to do anything positive. He certainly never considered doing anything for himself. How could he enjoy anything when his beloved Marjorie wasn't there to share it with him? He was only living half a life, he told me, and even when he had glimpses of enjoying himself again, he became overwhelmed with guilt. He felt that moving on was moving away from Marjorie, and was, therefore, a sign of disloyalty. Such was the turmoil of Lawrence's journey of grief.

It took him ages to begin to live again. With the support of good friends and his own inner resolve, he made it. And the sign and symbol of his making it? Well, you would guess it, wouldn't you? It was fulfilling his dream and going to the Grand Canyon. I must say I was surprised when I heard a couple of years after Marjorie's death that he was planning the trip, but delighted that he was motivated enough to do so. And I was even more delighted when I spoke to him on his return. He had planned the trip for himself, he said, but also for Marjorie. And, though they had never been there in reality, they had been there in their dreams, and it was, he said, the first time since her death that he had felt really close to her again. He cried for her when he was there. He talked to her when he was there. He missed her when he was there. And he was very, very close to her indeed when he was there.

So, fulfilling a dream in the Grand Canyon was, for Lawrence, the beginning of a new beginning. It might not have happened that way for everyone, but for Lawrence it had been the right thing to do. And why? Because he had finished a task and had found a comfort in so doing, and, as he told me himself, '… because, before she died, Marjorie had me promise that one day I would go. And, my God, I'm so glad I said I would.'

Notes
17 Robert Frost (1874–1963), from 'Stopping by woods on a snowy evening'.
18 Alexander Pope (1688–1744), from 'To Mr. Addison'.
19 Mary Lee Hall, 'Turn again to life'.

Charlie's wish

'You'll have a pipe-band at the funeral,' said Charlie,
'and the funeral people are not to wear black.
Everyone's to wear bright colours,' said Charlie,
'on my funeral day.'

'And the funeral director's not to wear a top hat.
Not even a suit would be my preference.
Bright shirts and flowery ties would be brilliant,' said Charlie,
'on my funeral day.'

'And no crying, mind.
It's to be a happy occasion.
For I'll be watching you,
so I will,
right enough,' said Charlie,
'on my funeral day.'

Well, Charlie,
we didn't have a pipe-band
on your funeral day.

Your wife said she couldn't stand the emotion.
And we didn't put 'No black, please' in the funeral notice –
so some of your old pals did wear black ties.
And one old guy even wore his medals,
on your funeral day.

And one of your daughters
wore a bright yellow blouse,
and the other one wore grey –
'Grey's the new black this season' she said –
because that's just them.
And we did ask the funeral director
about the shirt and tie bit,
because you asked us to.
And he just smiled –

a respectful, funeral-director kind of smile –
and we laughed out loud,
a breaking-the-embarrassed-tension kind of laugh,
a funny-picture-in-the-mind kind of laugh.
So it was top hat and pin-stripes as usual,
on your funeral day.

And it wasn't happy,
at least it wasn't for me –
even though the minister made it uplifting and helpful –
because you were dead
and that's why we were there.
And I cried buckets in the car.
And I hated you for going,
on your funeral day.

Did we do it right, Charlie?
Did we break a promise?
Did we do you justice
on your funeral day?

Would you mind our changes, Charlie?
Would you understand our reasons?
Would you know the purpose
on your funeral day?

Were you watching, Charlie?
Were you smiling on us?
Were you at one with us
on your funeral day?

'You'll have a pipe-band at the funeral,'
said Charlie.
But we didn't.
And we did it that way for Charlie
on his funeral day.

Will you

Will you promise to remember me when I am long since gone,
When you see me in the setting sun or hear me in our song?
Will you promise me you'll think of me and not forget too long?
Yes, I promise to remember when you're gone.

Will you promise to remember? Did you pick up all my cues –
How to work the tumble-dryer, and make casseroles and stews,
When the Council Tax needs paying, and how best to change a fuse?
Yes, I promise to remember when you're gone.

Will you promise to remember all the wonder of our days,
All the years we spent together – though they've vanished in a haze –
All those special, precious moments, all my funny little ways?
Yes, I promise to remember when you're gone.

Will you promise to remember what we talked about back then,
Of your favourite piece of music to be listened to again,
And the hymns you have to organise for singing at the crem?
Yes, I promise to remember when you're gone.

Will you promise to remember even when you cry and fret?
Will you hold me in your memory for a little longer yet?
For I'll live in your remembering – and in times when you forget ...
Yes, I promise to remember when you're gone.

Promises

I promise to be good.
Will you promise too?
   I promise I will love you.

I promise to forgive.
Will you promise too?
   I promise I will accept you.

I promise to be faithful.
Will you promise too?
   I promise to be with you.

I promise to the end.
Will you promise too?
   I promise to eternity.

I promise not to fail.
Will you promise too?
   My promise will never fail.

I promise what I promise.
Will you promise too?
   Yes, I promise too.

Five

Out of control

'Disguise fair nature with hard favour'd rage'
Shakespeare: 'Henry V'

'When angry, count to a hundred; when very angry, swear!'
Mark Twain: 'Pudd'nhead Wilson's Calendar'

A couple of years ago, along with two colleagues from the Iona Community, I was one of the co-leaders of a residential week in Iona Abbey on 'Living with Cancer'. I was there because of my experience as a hospice chaplain. Of the other two leaders, Jan ran a Day Hospice in Norfolk, and Zam had just completed courses of radiotherapy and chemotherapy following a mastectomy. Among the participants on the course there were those who were undergoing active treatment for cancer, those who were in remission having had surgery and various courses of treatment, those who were carers of cancer sufferers, and those who were involved with the caring professions.

Because of these different ways of engaging with the issue of living with cancer, we had decided to give everyone, including the leaders, a chance at the beginning of the week to share where we were with the issue and how, in our varying ways, cancer had touched our lives. So the first session – the 'getting to know each other' session – was entitled 'Joining the Club', the purpose being to try to find out how people saw themselves in this 'Cancer Club' – full members whether they had wanted to join or not; associate members involved at different levels; friends of the club, on the fringes, not fully in the centre of things; or simply interested bystanders who were intrigued and nothing more.

It was clear from that introduction – and it was a helpful thread that wove its way through the rest of our week together – that you cannot be a full member of this club, in the sense that we were exploring it, unless you had experienced cancer yourself. It wasn't sufficient that someone else's cancer had affected you, no matter how deeply. You could empathise; you could be committed; you could work with people with cancer; you could be in a family context where the spectre of cancer in the life of someone you loved loomed very large indeed. But unless you knew or had known what cancer was like in your own life, you were not and could not be a full member of the club.

It was a salutary reminder to a long-in-the-tooth hospice chaplain of where I stood in relation to the issue. A year before I'd been invited by my GP to participate in a study of prostate cancer in men over the age of fifty. If you agreed to be tested and it was discovered that you had cancer of the prostate, you would be 'randomised' as far as treatment was concerned – surgery, drug therapy or no treatment at all – to ascertain which approach was most effective in the long term. It was a Europe-wide study, and I agreed to be part of the research. So I had my blood-test done and I waited for the results, over Christmas and the New Year, I recall, and the wait was longer than I expected. Thankfully, my results were clear. But, as I now see it, my moments of apprehension as I waited made me realise that I was flirting with club membership. Would I be in or would I be out? How would I cope? Would I be 'cool' and controlled, or would I lose control? In effect, as far as membership of the club was concerned, I would have no choice, but my membership would clearly determine my future course of action. In many different ways it would fundamentally alter my life and the lives of those around me. So, my week on Iona, sharing with others who were living with cancer, helped me clarify what my real involvement with the cancer club actually was. I now knew where I stood.

My introduction to the bereavement club, however, was considerably less clear. My upbringing had been fairly typical of my generation. Not only was the reality of death offered in the sanitised fashion of the movies of the time, but bereavement was for adults; children were protected from it. I remember doing some work in counselling training well into my ministry and being invited to share my first experience of the death of someone close. I honestly couldn't remember any such experience at all in my growing-up years. Surely there had to be something. And then I remembered that when I was in primary school we had a family next door to us where three generations lived in the same house: two boys roughly my age, their parents and their granny. One day their granny was there. The next she wasn't. I know now that she must have died. Indeed I had that confirmed by my father many years later. But did I know it then? Not at all. While I was packed off to school, a funeral would have taken place, my mother and father would have been in black, curtains in the street would have been drawn, a black hearse would have stood outside the house, the local church would have been filled. But by the time I got back home, everything was as per normal, with not a word about funerals and death. And next-door-neighbours'-granny's absence? Never mentioned.

Yet when I qualified as a minister, and after two probationary years went on to work in my first parish in 1975 – at the ripe old age of twenty-six – I thought I knew about bereavement. After all, I had been well trained in theological college and had been tutored by able and experienced practical theologians and supervisors. I had been nurtured as a probationer minister by John Cook, a fantastic supervisor and colleague in Easterhouse in Glasgow, and had been well guided there by some wonderfully earthy and caring people in the congregation.

So, as a minister, I conducted funerals. I comforted bereaved people. I consoled those whose lives had been devastated by tragedy and loss. I offered hours of support, often to the detriment of time for my own family and myself. I believed myself to be – to use the image from our 'living with cancer' week on Iona – a fully engaged, paid-up, committed, attending, enthusiastic, office-bearing member of the bereavement club. I did not know how wrong I was until Talbot died.

Talbot Rooney was a friend and colleague. He was the Unit Organiser of a social-work agency in my first parish, 'The Family Service Unit', part of a national network of family orientated support teams in difficult inner-city and peripheral housing estates. I was chair of the unit management committee. I'd interviewed Talbot for the job, and, with his appointment, I knew that the unit and its work were in good hands. This big, gentle, quiet-spoken man was a pleasure to know and to work with. He was a good husband and father. He was an excellent colleague. He was a great man to call a friend.

Talbot contracted cancer in his early thirties, and, after a devastatingly short illness, died in the care of St Columba's hospice in Edinburgh. I visited him in the hospice in his final days. I was comfortable with that. After all, I had visited in the hospice many times in the past. I had often sat at the bedsides of dying people. My club membership was well intact! And so, once again, I cared, comforted, listened and supported. I'd done it all before.

The last time I saw Talbot was the day before he died. I know now what I did not know then, that this visit, and the aftermath of it, changed my life. I have often been asked what brought me into hospice chaplaincy. It began on that day.

Talbot was in a single room. Circumstances being what they were, I had time to be with him on my own. A nurse showed me into the room. It was clear that Talbot had lost a lot of ground since I had last seen him. Weight had fallen off this big man. His cheeks were sunken. His full beard which suited him so well in life just didn't look right now. His appearance had changed so much that I almost didn't recognise him as the man I'd known. I was both fascinated and appalled, fascinated by the mystic beauty of the bone structure of a skeletal form, and appalled at the wastage in such a full and healthy face. Talbot's eyes were closed. I sat and watched him for a while. I didn't pray, or touch him, or speak. I was overcome with helplessness. And inside I was beginning to seethe with anger. I could feel it boiling up, tensing my stomach, reddening my face, and pumping my heart. Why is this man like this? Why is this man dying? Why this waste? Why a life of love and service soon to be no more? Why, God? Why my friend and colleague? Why Talbot?

I was feeling anger such as I had never felt before. Tears began to well up in my eyes, something with which I was not at all comfortable at that stage of my life. So I took my leave – very suddenly. I had to get out of there in case something exploded in me and I disgraced myself. So, with one wistful, tear-filled look of goodbye, I left a dying friend. The next I knew I was in the hospice car-park. And there I stood, clerical collar and all, and I screamed and screamed. I do not know who or what I was screaming at. I have no recollection of forming or uttering any words. I have no idea whether anyone heard or saw this strange sight. I do not know if I was following Mark Twain's maxim, 'When very angry, swear!'[20] But I know I screamed a cathartic scream, until my screaming was done.

What happened next, I simply do not remember. Talbot died the next day. I attended his funeral Mass and paid my respects to his family. But what did I do with my outburst? I buried it like so many other unresolved, unexplained experiences at that time. The Family Service Unit moved on and a replacement for Talbot was found. I moved on too, with more work of ministry to be done. But the memory remained, important but dormant in the recesses of my psyche. And it was only when I went back to revisit the incident in counselling some years later in an attempt to understand some of the influences on my life, and resolve their effect on the direction my life and ministry had taken, that I began to understand the importance of it for me. I came to see the screaming in the hospice car-park for what it certainly must have been. It was my initiation into membership of the club of those who are bereaved.

Oh, I'd had bereavements in my family before. And, of course, I'd officiated at the funeral of many a good person. So it wasn't that I'd had no experience of loss. But, with Talbot's death, and the image of his dying in that last day of his life, death and loss were really affecting me for the very first time – not in my head with knowledge and understanding; not in my practice of ministry, bringing new skills and ideas; but in my heart, in my gut, in my very being – that core of self, that angry, boiling-over, lashing-out, screaming, vulnerable, out-of-control self. This was me reacting to loss – me, the real me, not the minister me, the controlled, capable, supportive minister me, but the me who could feel hurt, and pain, and devastation, and out-of-control anger. Was it a me I liked? Certainly not. Was it a me that mattered? Oh, yes indeed.

So I can trace my engagement with bereavement issues, a real engagement with them, membership of the club if you like, back to that moment. But even more importantly, I can trace my understanding of the feelings of loss back to that moment of being out of control. I am thankful, therefore, that I have been able to go back and revisit Talbot's death and learn from it. Sadly, I have worked with many people over the years who have had their 'out of control' moments and who have found them destructive, or who have buried them so deeply that they can have no ownership of them in a constructive way, and have, therefore, not learned from their experiences.

There are times when it is right to be out of control. How else are we supposed to react? Shakespeare has King Henry make this great, rousing pre-battle speech[21]:

Once more unto the breach, dear friends, once more;
Or close the wall up with your English dead!
In peace there's nothing so becomes a man

As modest stillness and humility:
But when the blast of war blows in our ears,
Then imitate the action of the tiger;
Stiffen the sinews, summon up the blood,
Disguise fair nature with hard-favour'd rage.

Whatever was the 'modest stillness' of peace, when sinews were stiffened and the blood was up it would inevitably have to be overtaken by a different and terrible aspect. 'Disguise fair nature with hard favour'd rage,' Henry reminds his troops.

When the blast of the war, the turmoil, the devastation of bereavement 'blows in our ears', it is no different. To deny the rage is to deny the reality. To deny the reality is not to feel the loss. Not to feel the loss is not to live.

In their book *The Love Which Heals*[22], the Wild Goose Resource Group offer this little story.

Bessie Brown was old when she told the story of how, in the 50s, she had gone to a funeral. A woman had been killed in a car crash, leaving three young children and a distraught husband. The mourners had gathered in the house, round the coffin, waiting for the pastor to come and say prayers. Eventually, the door swung open, and in swooped the pastor proclaiming, 'She is not here! She is risen!' 'I just wanted to punch him in the face,' said Bessie. 'We were not in any doubt of the general resurrection of the dead. We needed to ask, why her, and why now, and what's going to happen to the children.'

And the story is followed by this comment:

And God is big enough. God is big enough to take our anger, our questions, our doubt as well as our guilt. And perhaps unless we say 'Why?', or 'Where are you, God?', or 'Who is there to understand?' we will never be able to sing 'Hallelujah!'

The question 'Why?' in the face of suffering and death is not a question which requires or, indeed, expects an answer, even though it is followed by a question-mark. It has to be seen for what it is: a cry of pain, a cry of devastation, of sorrow, of hopelessness, of anguish. If that is how we feel, then that is where we have to begin. If our fair nature is overtaken by 'hard favour'd rage', then so be it. And the acknowledgement of that within ourselves, and the accepting of that in the suffering of others, has to be the beginning of healing. Yes, with Bessie, I think I would want to punch the pastor as well, and maybe that would have been a healing moment for me too.

If, then, the question 'Why?' is a cry of pain, how are we to deal with it? Maybe this image will help. Imagine yourself taking a child to a swing-park or playground. You trust the child to be sensible and play safely, and so you settle down on the bench at the side with your book, keeping an occasional eye on the playing child. After a while, as you've become engrossed in your book, suddenly the air is broken by an ear-piercing scream and you see the child running towards you with a badly grazed knee. You know immediately what to do. You place the book calmly on the bench and, once the child has come close to you, you ask her to sit cross-legged on the ground while you give her a simple but detailed lecture on the physiology of pain, and how the brain understands the signals sent to it by the nerve-endings at the site of the graze. No? Perhaps not. Maybe, then, you offer her some insights into the meaning of suffering, quoting C.S. Lewis or Emanuel Kant on the way, and adding in your own personal philosophy. No? So you might suggest that she is exhibiting an expression of inner feelings, aligned to some under-standing of Transactional Analysis or Gestalt Counselling. No, of course not. Instead, you throw the book aside, open your arms wide, gather the child up on your knee, and hold her until the screaming and sobbing subside. You offer her your instinctive compassion, the embrace of your love. The screaming child does not wish to hear or would not understand the reasons for her pain. She needs and cries out for reassurance. The damaged child does not seek or will not expect conclusions or comment on her grazed knee. She needs and longs for comfort and consolation.

It is no different with the pain, the rage, the cries, metaphorical and real, of the devastation of loss. Those who are bereaved need reassurance not reasons, comfort not comment, acceptance not explanations. They need to be held, physically and emotionally, in an embrace of love and understanding and not be pushed away. The cry of pain that is the 'Why?' in the face of death needs to be offered the openness of our love in response and not the cleverness of our knowledge and ideas.

The Book of Lamentations in the Bible is a collection of five poems lamenting the destruction of Jerusalem in 586 BC and its aftermath of ruin and exile. These poems are used by Jews in worship on the annual days of fasting and mourning. In their expression of loss and brokenness they encapsulate something of the depth of despair which bereavement brings:

Like a widow ... all night long she cries;
Tears run down her cheeks.
Of all her former friends,
not one is left to comfort her.[23]

That is why my eyes are overflowing with tears.
No one can comfort me;
no one can give me courage.[24]

My eyes are worn out with weeping;
My soul is in anguish.
I am exhausted with grief ...
No one has ever suffered like this.[25]

Of course there is hope. In the book of Lamentations, as in other writings, hope is expressed and experienced by those who are living with and have come through the devastation of their loss. In the experiences of those who have lived with bereavement and those who support them, hope is a sustaining feature. But just as the Chinese proverb reminds us that the greatest journey begins with a single step, so we have to understand where the journey of bereavement begins, and that is often with the out-of-control cry of devastation, before hope can ever be expressed or understood. When former friends have abandoned you in your grief; when the whole world appears to be against you; when your eyes are overflowing with tears; when your soul is in anguish; when you are worn out with weeping; when no one has ever suffered like this ... that is when your cries need to be heard, and that is where compassion and understanding have to begin.

When I was a young minister, trying to make sense of the troubles and anguish people have to deal with in their lives, I did my best to minister to them and help them make sense of their woes. I hope I did OK and didn't make any glaring mistakes. But I know now what I didn't really know then: that I knew 'nothing about nothing' (as someone was honest enough to tell me once ...) and that I had an awful lot to learn. Consequently, very early on, I was horrified by an incident I was witness to, an incident I was quite out of my depth to understand and know how to deal with.

I was conducting a funeral service in a family home prior to going to the interment at the local cemetery. The coffin of the deceased, the mother of a big family, was in the bedroom – a largely uncommon tradition now but still familiar to working-class families and many rural communities thirty years ago – and once people had said their final goodbyes we were gathering the mourners together in the living-room for the service, at the same time allowing the funeral director to close the coffin and take it out to the hearse.

I was just about to start the service in the crowded front room when I heard the wailing and the screaming. 'No! No! Don't close the lid on ma mammy. No! Don't take her away! No! NO!' It was heart-rending and it was very, very scary. Here was anguish with all of its ferocity right there in a family home. The mourners rushed from the room towards the source of the screams. And there, in the bedroom, was one of the teenage daughters of the family, holding on to the coffin, kicking out at the funeral director, trying to lift her mother, and screaming and shouting with rage. The ensuing scene was like something out of a bad movie. Family members were trying to pull the young woman away. The dishevelled funeral director was far from his immaculate best. The coffin shroud had been torn. And mother was lying at a somewhat undignified and abnormal angle.

Eventually order was regained and we gathered again in the living room, leaving the funeral director to restore his personal equilibrium and that of the unfortunate deceased. I have no idea how I conducted the service, what I said or what I did. I had simply been blown away by what had happened. The young lady moaned and wailed all the way through my inadequate words of consolation. Occasionally others joined in with their own vocal expressions of distress. There were times when I found it hard to make myself heard. It was no different at the cemetery. The still hysterical daughter had to be physically restrained from jumping into the grave once the coffin had been lowered down. It was – and remains in my mind nearly thirty years later – an absolute nightmare.

I know now that such a public expression of anguish, being so out of control at a death, is not untypical. I know now because I can add to this story many tales of other out-of-control people over the years who have not been able to hold anything back in the public expression of their grief. And I know now because I've been there myself. I've been out of control too.

I learned an old Spiritual some years ago, where the words sum up something of that devastation. We are rightly offended by death, and, before we can reflect rationally, hold to cherished beliefs or make sense of fond memories, the devastation might simply be too much to hold at bay.

I was standing by my window,
On one cold and cloudy day
When I saw that hearse come rolling
For to carry my mother away

Will the circle be unbroken
By and by, Lord, by and by
There's a better home a-waiting
In the sky, Lord, in the sky

I said to that undertaker
Undertaker please drive slow
For this lady you are carrying
Lord, I hate to see her go

Will the circle...

Oh, I followed close behind her
Tried to hold up and be brave
But I could not hide my sorrow
When they laid her in the grave

Will the circle...

I went back home, my home was lonesome
Missed my mother, she was gone
All of my brothers, sisters crying
What a home so sad and lone

Will the circle...

We sang the songs of childhood
Hymns of faith that made us strong
Ones that mother May-Belle taught us
Hear the angels sing along

Will the circle...

Before any exploration of hope and strength could be found, there was a sorrow that could not and should not be hidden, a loneliness that was painful, and a home that was sad and empty.

Such knowledge of the feelings of devastation around a death may make understanding easier. But it doesn't make the events easier to cope with, for there are still accepted norms and customs, and restrained and reserved behaviour comes as part of the package. So, on the occasions when people are out of control, and break the conventions, and give vent to their feelings, we are disquieted or horrified to different degrees. We would prefer not to witness such public spectacles of grief. If people are to be out of control, let them keep it private, or if not private but in a hospice car-park, let it not impinge on the welfare or disturb the equilibrium of anyone else.

When my grandfather died, everyone at the funeral parlour and the crematorium was controlled and dignified. Everyone, that is, except the barmaid from my grandfather's local, who, outside the crematorium after the service was over, was sobbing and wailing uncontrollably. I remember the looks of disdain on people's faces when they saw her and heard her display of grief. I remember my mother turning away in disgust. I remember feeling appalled myself, and thinking, 'For God's sake, woman, you were only his barmaid. Get a grip of yourself!'

Perhaps we should be more understanding. Of course we are disturbed when conventions are broken. But might we not be more tolerant if we see the extremes of grief for what they are: a powerful expression of the devastation of loss? Even barmaids know what loss means. Being out of control can be OK if we understand where it is coming from. After all, if we lived in another culture, being out of control, wailing, screaming, moaning, shouting, and the like, would be the norm, the expected behaviour in grief. And not to express grief in such ways would be considered disrespectful, a dishonouring of the dead, and an inadequate expression of loss.

All of this makes me encouraged by my hospice staff's reaction to a recent incident in one of our wards. A lady had come into the hospice as an emergency admission during the morning; she had deteriorated rapidly at home and her husband did not want her to die in the house. She was very poorly when she arrived with us, and we did our best to settle her and to be supportive of the family members who had accompanied her. So, for a few hours, things were reasonably controlled as several members of the team offered practical and emotional support to a struggling family, and family members were understanding and supportive of each other.

Early in the afternoon, many in the hospice heard the screams. Some thought it was a patient in pain. But those who had been involved knew it for what it was – the devastation of a grieving husband and daughter when death had come to their family. The screams did not last long, but they had affected the whole place. Even those working in offices on the floor above knew what was going on. It was the talk of the building. On the ward, the out-of-control people had been supported, hugged, comforted, affirmed in their devastation. That's what would be hoped for and, indeed, expected from caring and understanding relatives and staff. But it was the reactions of the other people, those not directly involved, that interested and encouraged me. For not once did I hear criticism or judgement. Not once did I hear the suggestion that such out-of-control behaviour was in any way inappropriate. Instead there was tolerance, sympathy, and, dare I suggest, fellow-feeling.

Who knows, maybe that's how people I'd never met or never knew about reacted to my screams in the hospice car-park when Talbot died. Maybe they knew what I still had to learn, that I needed to be what I needed to be, out of control in my grief. Maybe, out of sight but very real, there was tolerance, sympathy and fellow-feeling from them too, for me.

Notes

[20] Mark Twain (1835–1910), from 'March' in 'Pudd'nhead Wilson's Calendar'.

[21] William Shakespeare, *Henry V*, Act III, Scene i.

[22] 'The Love Which Heals – a service of grieving & gratitude for those who have been recently bereft', John L. Bell (Wild Goose Resource Group, 2000).

[23] Lamentations 1:1,2.

[24] Lamentations 1:16.

[25] Lamentations 12:11,13.

Sainsbury's

It happened in Sainsbury's.
Shopping had to be done
for me.
'Keep going,' they'd said.
and so my going to Sainsbury's that first time
was my necessity.
'You have to eat.'
So it was the time,
the list,
the furrowed brow,
the hasty rush,
the basket –
not the trolley needed now
to shop for one,
the simple things –
no complicated thoughts around the ready-meals,
no choice,
just shop and go.

And almost done,
I went to pay,
and then I heard –
the laughing voice
two aisles away,
the laughter of two voices now,
too loud,
too public here,
this sharing of a mutual joy,
the spontaneous burst of pleasure there,
intruding on my private shopping pilgrimage.

How angry I became!
What right,

what right have they,
what right have they, in here,
what right have they, in here, to laugh?
What right have they, in here, to laugh out loud?
Do they not know?
Do they not understand my purpose here,
to shop – alone –
and quickly go,
escape this public chore,
to shop for me alone, and not for us?
Should they not also mourn for you?
Should the whole world,
and Sainsbury's,
not be a place of silent grief
now you are gone?
Do they not care?
Should they not also shop with furrowed brow
and silent baskets
while I mourn for you?

It happened in Sainsbury's,
in raging anger's pain,
in floods of tears by a lonely trolley park,
I knew,
I knew
that grief for you would be a lonely thing,
and laughter in a Sainsbury's aisle would tell the truth,
'You're on your own,'
while we can laugh out loud
two aisles away
in Sainsbury's.

I began this chapter by recounting the effect on me of a week on Iona, sharing in the journey of life and hope with people affected by 'the cancer club'. This poem was written during that week and used in worship in Iona Abbey, as it encapsulated many of the longings that emerged for all of us at that time.

Acceptance

Accept me as I am,
for this is me, it's all I have to offer.
Accept me as I am,
for what I am is all that I can be.
Accept me as I am,
this gift I bring is all I have to give you.
Accept this life,
the gift I bring is me.

So see me as I am,
for this is me, though not what you might wish for.
And know me as I am,
though what I am has changed the me you see.
And love me as I am,
this gift is still the gift I have to offer.
This gift is life,
the life that's still in me.

Believe me as I am,
for this is me, with new truth worth the sharing.
Believe me as I am,
though what I am comes over differently.
Believe me as I am,
this gift is one that's worthy of accepting.
The old has gone,
the new me is still me.

Understand me as I am,
this is still me, though words come over wrongly.
And hear me as I am
when boldness makes me speak confidently.
So cope with what I am,
this gift I've found that's lain long undiscovered
has given voice
to that unspoken me.

Do I know who I am,
this me that's new and craves a new acceptance?
Can I love what I am,
though what I am's not what I want to be?

If I am what I am,
this gift needs you to help me to discover,
just who I am,
the me that has to be.

So hold me as I am,
for this is me, the me that's worth embracing.
Console me as I am,
for what I am still needs your constancy.
Enfold me as I am,
this gift I give is worth more than rejection.
The need remains –
to love the me that's me.

I rage

I rage at God,
And in my angry shouts I hate his will.
I scream at God,
And in my wails I will disturb his rest.
I rant at God,
And in my raving prayers would have him hear.
I rail at God,
And in my tears and cries I doubt his way.
I curse at God,
And in my lost control offend his ear.
I am with God
What I must be, for now, for this.
I am with God,
Ev'n now, with rage, ev'n now, with God,
I am with God.
Please God, I pray you understand.

Six

Rituals and celebrations

'Thrift, thrift, Horatio! The funeral bak'd meats
Did coldly furnish forth the marriage tables.'
Shakespeare: 'Hamlet'

'Be happy while y'er leevin,
For y'er a lang time deid.'
Anon: Scottish motto for a house

When my friend Farquhar died, one of the elderly men who was a
close friend in the church where Farquhar was a minister, on learning of the death, went straight home and changed into his dark suit,
white shirt and black tie as a mark of respect. He was immediately in
mourning for the death of his friend. I asked him later why he had
done this. 'Because,' he said, 'I would have felt I'd done something
wrong if I hadn't. It was just the right thing to do.'

A few years ago my wife and I were in Italy with some friends.
Visiting Pisa, we were approaching the leaning tower when a minibus
drew up and decanted a dozen or so matronly ladies, all dressed in
black and various shades of grey. 'Widows,' my friend whispered in my
ear. 'How can you tell?' I asked, naively. 'Because they're wearing
clown's hats and bright-red pyjamas, daftie!' he replied. But of course
he was right in his identification of the widow-women. For widows
here wore the blacks and greys that widows should wear, so that we
could be aware of their mourning and their loss.

When Elisha the biblical prophet was faced with the death of
Elijah, his friend and mentor – a fascinating story which I'll look at
further in the final chapter – the Bible story tells us that he took his
own clothes and tore them apart, right there in full view of everyone else. Nothing odd in that whatsoever. It was expected. It was

understood. It was the right thing to do. It was, if you like, the black tie or the widow's weeds of his day.

In all of these circumstances, people were expressing, in their own personal understanding and within their cultural norms, what bereavement meant to them. A public expression of loss was important in biblical times, in Catholic Italy, and for an old Presbyterian man in a secular society. In their culture, what we would now call 'in days gone by', other people would have fully understood, accepted and participated in that process, for such were the norms their society lived by. Yet in the two cases in which I was personally involved, I had to check out what was happening because it was unfamiliar to me. (And if someone had started to take his clothes and tear them apart in front of me and other people … well, I'm not sure *what* I would have done!) Of course I knew people wore black to funerals. But in the run-up to the funeral, and for some considerable time afterwards? That was new to me.

I suspect it will be like that for a lot of people nowadays. Whatever was normal behaviour when I began my ministry thirty years ago has largely been forgotten. People don't close their curtains or lower their blinds any more to indicate that there's been a death in their house or in their street. The crematorium has largely taken the place of the graveside burial. Cortèges are less common in the cities now, with the hearse often waiting at the crematorium gates or the coffin even being in place in the crematorium chapel before the mourners arrive. People choose to have their loved one 'viewed' at the funeral director's rest rooms and less frequently at home. Men don't doff their hats as a hearse drives by. Seldom would people come back to the house for a wake, choosing instead to go on to a hotel for a more formal gathering for refreshments. The days of the cold sausage roll, the curled-up ham sandwich and the accompanying 'funeral bak'd meats'[26], whether for reasons of thrift or otherwise, are sadly numbered. I could go on, but I suspect you can relate to the issue. Death has become sanitised. The events of the early stages of loss are controlled and organised, the funeral director 'undertaking' more than ever before, taking on all the planning, and thus largely replacing an awareness within families of what is expected or understood according to accepted cultural norms.

Of course, one has glimpses from time to time of what has been. When I conducted a graveside funeral service on the island of Jura off the West Coast of Scotland some years ago and completed the interment, I was surprised to see the funeral director and his men moving quietly among the mourners in the cemetery car-park with glasses of whisky, oatcakes and small blocks of cheese. When I enquired about this practice, so strange to my city eyes, I was told by the island funeral director, 'Aye, well, you being a city minister may not know about this. Here we stick to the old customs. In days gone by people would have walked from the ends of the island to attend a funeral in this very graveyard. And this, a gift from the family, was their sustenance for the long journey home. Well, well now,' he continued, 'but things are not what they were, for nowadays, you see, there are some people who are getting very cosmopolitan and going to the local hotel.' I, for one, was happy to be among the non-cosmopolitans on that day, for I recall the old-custom sustenance being very welcome indeed!

For a minister, however, the most obvious change in the approach to death centres around the preparation and conducting of the funeral service. There is in Scotland, and I suspect elsewhere, an increase in secular or humanist funerals, with, for example, the Humanist Society of Scotland having in place a series of Funeral Advisors throughout the country. There is an equal increase in the number of 'DIY' funerals, at which various people offer and coordinate the tributes, readings, music and the like that go to make up the event. And there is, therefore, an increasing desire to have ministers of all denominations work with families in this secularisation and

DIY-ness of the funeral business. Gone are the days when 'You'll know best, minister' is the only guidance one gets from a family. The standard 'Book of Common Order' service is no longer deemed sufficient. To refer to the deceased only as 'our dear departed brother' is no longer enough – if it was ever of any use! And the crematorium organist is in danger of being superseded by the chapel attendant's ever-expanding role as DJ, as he or she attempts to fulfil requests for various selections of music.

I once talked with a man who had decided that he didn't want a funeral service at all, but, instead, wanted a massive firework display, 'the kind they have at the end of the Edinburgh Festival', he explained. The trouble was, he discovered that if you were planning a firework display of that magnitude you had to get permission from Air Traffic Control at Edinburgh Airport because of the potential disruption of aircraft flight-paths. And to do that he needed to tell them the exact day and time of the event. Organised though he undoubtedly was, that information was not yet to hand!

This is not the place in which to explore 'funerals I have known' or to present a treatise on 'what makes a good funeral'. But it does seem to me that it is not unhealthy that people are drawing on their own cultural expressions in the planning and presentation of a funeral, seeking to create an event which works for them, which is informed by their cultural norms, and which, therefore, can provide a platform for the beginning of the bereavement journey. The funeral is extremely important in the grieving process. It is a bridge between what has been and what will be. If the bridge is built well and is strong and stable – in other words, if the funeral is a positive experience for those who are present – then the transition for those who grieve will be made with confidence. If the bridge is badly built and shaky due to a lack of care and sensitivity – in other words, if the funeral has lived up to the very low expectations many people have of such events – then the mourners will cross it filled with apprehension, and will make a very uncertain start on the next stage of the journey of loss.

When my granny's sister died, I attended the funeral at the church with the family. It was a fairly bland occasion, it seemed to me, with the minister largely doing it 'by the book' – apart, that is, from one thing. The old lady was a great collector of money for the church and charities. She didn't get out of the house much latterly, so the way she gathered her cash was to insist that everyone who came to the house emptied their pockets or purses of their pennies and two-pences – what she called your 'brown money' – and placed their loose change in a jar on the window ledge, and jar after jar would ultimately end up benefiting the local church or chosen charitable enterprises. During the funeral thanksgiving prayer, the minister said two things that weren't 'in the book'. Firstly, he called the old lady by her family name, Aillie rather than Ellen – for as far as I was aware no one ever knew her as anything else – and, secondly, he gave thanks to God for her commitment to collecting 'her brown money'. And what was the talk afterwards as the mourners gathered in the old lady's house for their 'funeral bak'd meats'? Yes, it was 'He called her Aillie' and 'He mentioned her brown money.' It was the buzz of the family. It had made the funeral work. It had been the real Aillie with the real brown money who had been remembered.

So it is more and more with the preparation of funerals today. Ask the crematorium staff and they'll give you the top ten tunes played at funerals. A recent survey found that Robbie Williams's 'Angels' was the top choice. Tina Turner's 'Simply the best' is up there. 'My way' by Elvis or Frank Sinatra will figure highly. 'Everybody hurts' by REM, 'Wind beneath my wings', 'I will always love you', 'Always look on the bright side of life' – and the list goes on. Amongst possible readings, Henry Scott Holland's 'Death is nothing at all' – often requested but desperately bad theology and bereavement insight in the way it's presented, and not the way Scott Holland would have wished it at all – would be close to the top. (The focus on this particular piece is an interesting phenomenon, and one that has caused headaches for many ministers. My own reflections on it are unfolded in more personal detail at the end of this chapter.) And, of course, there's the homespun poetry, the lines of doggerel, the forced rhymes, the badly scanned stanzas, the twee sentimentality, excruciating to some ears, yet offered with deep sincerity and loved by everyone present.

None or all of these would be my cup of tea. And yet for many people, in the devastation of their loss, they work. Well planned, sincerely felt, realistically used, they work. And they work for three reasons: firstly, because they represent the 'brown money' syndrome, giving people ownership of and involvement with the ritual; secondly, they emphasise the spiritual over the religious, and that seems to me to be a better response to a society and individuals within it who are searching for meaning than to impose meaningless religion on them just for the sake of it; and thirdly, it gives a solid platform to bereavement, not necessarily provided by all funerals in the past.

I once took the funeral service of Deeko, a young man who died in our hospice and who was an out-and-out rogue. In and out of prison since he was a teenager, his body had been the victim of much personal abuse. And at the age of 40 he was struck down by cancer. He had asked me himself if I would conduct the service. 'Wull you do ma thing,' he asked me one day, 'yon thing ye huv to dae after somewan's deid ...' 'A funeral?' I responded. 'Aye, that's right,' Deeko replied, and he told me he wanted me to do 'his thing' because he felt I would 'tell the truth' and wouldn't make him out to be any saint (and the more I got to know Deeko, the less chance there was of that!). He wanted the funeral to be 'real' for his mates. So, I worked hard at the funeral – with Deeko himself before he died and with my own preparation afterwards – seeking to be true to so many conflicting pulls on my integrity. It wasn't easy, but it was worth it.

I remember Deeko telling me that, because he was so chuffed

with our care, there had to be a collection for the hospice at the funeral. He suggested two things about this collection: first, that it would be best for someone to stand guard over the collection plate as some of his mates would be more inclined to remove money from the plate than to add to it; and, second, that I was to insist to the assembled company that they 'put all their money in the plate before they spend it on bevvy!' I suggested to Deeko that while the first would be easy to organise, the second might be difficult for me to say, in these words, at any rate. 'Tell them ah said so,' he insisted. So, I did, and there was £685 in the plate – and none taken out! Deeko obviously knew his mates better than I did. As far as the funeral service – 'yon thing ye huv to dae after somewan's deid' – was concerned, I think we must have pretty well got it right, because at the end Deeko's aunt, who was, I discovered, a deeply religious woman, said through her tears, 'Thank you for making a religious service so meaningful,' closely followed by a comment from one of Deeko's mates – broken nose, skin-head, jeans and T-shirt – who grunted, 'That wiz great, pal. Just right fur Deeko. An' it wuznae religious at a'.'

Funerals, and the search for rituals which work, which matter, and which express what needs to be expressed, are, therefore, very important. I would be happy to be remembered as 'the man who did a good funeral', not because I seek praise, but because we have been able to create an event which is, for those who grieve, the solid bridge between the death and the bereavement journey.

There are many stories in my mind as I write this. Let me share one which still means a lot to me. I'm grateful for the family's permission to recount it here. Davy Steele was a musician and a member of the Battlefield Band. Davy's wife, Patsy and their wee boy, Jamie, were the lights of his life. His musical career with the band had started to take off. And Davy had a brain tumour. I got to know Davy very well during his time in the hospice. By then Davy couldn't speak, far less sing. But he could certainly communicate with his eyes. I learned later from various people that he had been a real character. And his eyes still spoke of that. Eric Bogle told me it was just as well Davy could speak only with his eyes, for if I'd known him when he spoke with his mouth I would have found that I could hardly get a word in edgeways! Patsy, Jamie, family members, and lots of folk from the music business were regular visitors.

It pained me to see such a talented man in such a state. Music has always been important to me, and the kind of music Davy played is among my favourite styles. I was filled with questions about the 'why' of this waste of a life, and deeply affected by his dying. I still am. I'm looking forward to a jam session with Davy when we get to that great Ceilidh in the sky. Whatever happens after you die, I want to be where Davy is.

Robert Burns wrote these words as a tribute to his friend, William Muir of Tarbolton Mill:

An honest man here lies at rest
As e'er God with His image blest:
The friend of man, the friend of truth,
The friend of age and guide of youth;
Few hearts like his − with virtues warm'd,
Few heads with knowledge so inform'd:
If there's another world, he lives in bliss;
If there is none, he made the best of this.

This is one of the most inclusive readings I know and I use it regularly at funeral services. By being so inclusive and so honest, it is, therefore, one of the most effective. What happens after you die? I have absolutely no idea! I have hopes, I have beliefs, I have important thoughts, I have my own faith, but I cannot say that I know. But I can say of people like Davy, *If there's another world, he lives in bliss; if there is none, he made the best of this*, and that's good enough for me.

In *The Love which Heals*[27], John Bell tells this story:

When Jack Robertson was very small, he used to ask his grandmother about heaven. 'Heaven?' she would reply, 'I'll tell you about heaven. When you get to heaven there will be three surprises in store for you. The first will be seeing all the people who are there. The second will be realising all the people who aren't there. And the third will be discovering that you are there yourself.'

I was chuffed to bits to be invited by Patsy to conduct Davy's funeral service. We planned the service together with family members in Davy and Patsy's home, surrounded by the musical instruments that were their life. When it came to the service itself, all the elements of it worked. Fellow members of the Battlefield Band played. A broad Scots reading was offered. A tribute from a musician colleague was read. A modern song was sung. A personal tribute was read by Davy's sons, David and Mark. And we listened to a track of Davy singing. It was a special occasion, and one which I was privileged to be part of.

I remember coming to the lectern at the crematorium after Davy had been piped in, looking at the huge gathering of people, and saying, 'What a gig!' I did not mean that in any disrespectful way then, or as I share it now, but it indicated how really important this event was to all those who had gathered together. Yes, it was remembering Davy. Yes, it was paying tribute to a real character. But it was more. It was drawing out lessons, the eternal truths which such occasions allow us to focus upon, perhaps like never before. And it was also about providing a launching pad, an important bridge, for Patsy, Jamie, and Davy's family and friends for their future. Get it right and they have something to build on. Get it wrong, and you make the platform, the bridge, even more shaky than it was before.

During his illness, Davy's family had set up a website for contributions, stories and words of comfort and support. There were offerings from all over the world. After the funeral there were some really positive comments about how it had gone, with people saying they had been helped by the occasion. Such direct feedback isn't that common, but, my God, it makes it worthwhile. Dick Gaughan, one of my heroes in the Scottish music scene, said he'd found the service helpful. I can think of no higher praise than that.

Among my own offerings at the funeral were the words of James Keelaghan[28], asking people to ponder their mortality, to think about what matters in their life, and while they are well enough to do so.

A nephew once asked me when he was quite young,
'Who dies?' I said, 'Everyone dies.'
No use denying it, one day you're done,
Oh, everyone dies.
Princes and paupers, there's no one immune,
and no one who'll escape their demise.
So you'd better make use of each day that you're given –
Oh, everyone dies.

Now people have pondered this time and again,
Who dies? Everyone dies.
We suspect that we're more than mere mortal remains.
Oh, everyone dies.
Wise men and prophets they've all had their say
on the nature of their afterlives.
But in case there's no beer there we'll have one more round!
Oh, everyone dies.

Your time may be short or your time may be long.
Who dies? Everyone dies.
But it's going to happen as sure as you're born.
Oh, everyone dies.
Friends and relations and all we hold dear
will one day pass to the other side.
So we'd better embrace them as long as they're here.
Oh, everyone dies.

And Davy's contribution? Well, he's still making his contribution, to me certainly, to Patsy and Jamie, David, Mark and their sister, Krysty, along with the wider family, and, I'm sure, to many other people whom he touched with his music and his personality. But his offering at the funeral is worth recording again here. It was a song he'd written for Patsy, and one that was chosen for the funeral by Mark, Davy's younger son. So Davy was very much involved with his own ritual. He, with the others, had made it work. [29]

Every time I watch you go away,
Like a swallow flying South,
Cold feelings in my soul again,
Frozen words in my mouth;
A sudden burst of clumsy movements,
Then I watch you slowly fade.
Our partings are the hardest moments,
With all the things we've left unsaid.

Long hellos and short goodbyes,
And in between the time just flies.
It gets lonely, heaven knows,
Waiting for these long hellos.

Slow nights are those we spend alone,
Knowing it's to be this way,
Counting hours, counting shimmering stars,
Watching dark skies turn to grey.
Those days we spend together
It seems we're always chasing time –
That goes so slow when you are everyone's
And goes too fast when you're just mine.

And if I found that I could do it all again
I wouldn't change a single thing,

For I would swim an ocean of tears
Just to hear my swallow sing.

Long hellos and short goodbyes,
And in between the time just flies.
It gets lonely, heaven knows,
Waiting for these long hellos.

My wife recently attended the funeral service of her friend's father. Bill was a likeable and gregarious man who had outlived his wife, Nona, by a number of years. The funeral service was introduced and closed with some piano music on the crematorium CD system, some music from the shows. It was Nona herself playing the piano, music recorded some years before, played as a comfort in a family home long after she had died, and now played at her husband's funeral. My wife told me it was as if Nona was there, and that she was now having the chance to grieve for Nona and Bill together.

A hospice chaplain colleague shared with me recently an account of a funeral he had conducted where he had used the 'Water bugs and dragonflies' story[30]. If you're not familiar with this short but profound story, get yourself a copy of it, for it is a visual and deeply meaningful insight into what dying is about. The chaplain had invited numerous children of the extended family to the front of the crematorium to act out the story as it was being read. So some played one insect and some another, and, through the enthusiasm of little children, and a visual portrayal of eternal truths, a message was shared and remembered.

In these and other ways, rituals and celebrations begin to work again, and, if carefully handled and sensitively delivered, they can be the bridge that people need from one stage of a life to another. Let me close with a personal story and a lesson learned. My father, of whom more later, was not a particularly demonstrative man. Discussions with him about planning a funeral, and even less planning his own, were not on! However, given my own line of work, and my recollections of my mother's death some years before and how unprepared the family were for that, I was always keen to find out from my dad what his wishes might be.

One day when he was spending a holiday with us, we were in the kitchen having a coffee with the TV on as background noise. Suddenly, my dad turned round, for he had heard a hymn tune on the TV that had make him prick up his ears. It was the lovely, haunting Irish melody 'Slane', for the hymn 'Be thou my vision, O Lord of my heart'. 'That's the hymn we used to sing on church parades when I was in the Air Force during the War,' my dad whispered. 'It's always been my favourite. It's the kind of hymn I'd like sung at my funeral.' And, given that the moment was right, I asked, tentatively, 'And are there any others you'd like as well?' 'Aye, there are ... "I to the hills" and "What a friend we have in Jesus" will do just fine.' And the moment was over. A little later I slipped upstairs and wrote down the titles of these three hymns in the back cover of my own hymn book. And they were there when they were needed as we were preparing for my dad's funeral service many years later.

My granny was quite wrong when she would say, 'Dinnae talk about death, son. It might make it happen quicker ...' Let us see death for what it is, an integral part of life. 'Who dies? Everyone dies!' Let's not push it to the margins, leave it sanitised, talk about it in whispers. Death has become for us what sex was to the Victorians – you know it's around, but you don't talk about it in polite company! So, if we can, let's talk about death, and ideas and suggestions about funerals too, not in a morbid, it'll-make-it-happen-quicker kind of way, but in an open, preparatory way. Let it be a help to those who are left after a death to begin their bereavement aright by creating a ritual and celebration that works. Write things down. Keep them safe. Know where they are, for you never know when you will need them, and when, like a scribbled note in the back cover of a hymn book, they will help in the creation of a ritual or celebration that will really, really matter.

Notes

26 William Shakespeare, *Hamlet*, Act I, scene i.

27 *The Love Which Heals, op cit.*

28 'Who dies?' written by James Keelaghan, © and ℗ 1999, Tranquilla Music (SOCAN), from the album *Road* by James Keelaghan.

29 From the CD *Chasing Shadows* by Davy Steele, FMS 2073, published by Temple Records.

30 *Waterbugs and Dragonflies: Explaining Death to Young Children* by Doris Stickney, Continuum, 2002.

Conducting funeral services is never easy, especially being responsive to conflicting demands and expectations. This is my prayer for myself at times like these.

A prayer at a funeral

Dear God,
no words can say what's right,
no flowers can show what's true,
no black can offer light,
no tears, no churchy pew
can make what's bad come good again.

Dear God,
make silent thoughts my prayer,
make wreaths the song I sing,
make black a sign of care,
make tears an offering
when all seems bad, and grief brings pain.

Dear God,
there are no words you use,
there are no flowers you give,
no black, no church, no pews,
no tears, to make us live
and make what's bad come good again.

So, God,
speak in this silent time,
speak in this holy place,
banish the black with Light,
hold me in Love's embrace
when good breaks through the bad. Amen.

I have often been asked to use the words of the prayer of Canon Henry Scott Holland in funeral services, as a way of offering hope amidst the darkness of people's loss. Yet while I respect the reasons for which people choose this reflection, I have a growing sense of unease with its language and symbolism. Indeed, I am sure that Scott Holland himself would be equally uneasy at the way his meaningful words are often misinterpreted as a facile reassurance. The reflection begins, for example, with the assertion that 'Death is nothing at all', and while I can understand the Christian context in which these words were written, to say in a funeral service that you believe death is nothing is surely to belittle the pain and devastation people really feel. Equally, 'I have just slipped into the next room', '... just around the corner', and '... all is well', while offering hope and reassurance to some, can create confusion and a false reality for others. What follows, therefore, is not a counter to Scott Holland's words, but is simply my way of affirming the rightness of people's feelings, and the reassurance that to start with the reality of pain, far from making things worse, can actually be the beginning of a healing journey.

I'm dead

I'm dead,
no longer here to laugh and cry
and share with you our precious love.
In death
I have departed this so fragile life,
to be no more your true companion
on our eventful path
through cherished years
of life and love,
of learning and of growing,
of constant childlike joy
of our amazing gift of being together.

So be assured of this;
know I am dead;
understand I have departed;
I am gone from you.

This is the truth –
and no amount of softening words,
no euphemisms shared,
no clever prayers,
no reassurance, though indeed sincere,
can e'er erase this dreadful, harsh reality.

So, do not say or yet believe,
this death is nothing.
And do not feel or yet accept
that another corner turned,
another room explored,
will find me there.
And do not cry or yet in faith express
that all is well.

For is not this death our everything?
And is not this leave-taking
for now for ever?
And can the world not know and understand
that all is not well,
that nothing can be well,
that even God, in faith,
must now accept this pain,
this hellishness,
this devastating cry of woe?

So this I ask of you,
this plea I make to you who've loved

and lost the one whom you did love with all your heart;
this truth you have to know,
what now you have to do –
begin with this death.
Start from this loss,
this hopeless, painful loss;
begin with what you feel, and know, and understand
to be your own reality,
your awful, deep reality
that dawns for you so dark and overwhelming on this day of death.
And know, and hate that I am dead.
And feel your rage at my departing.

And then,
and only then will you begin again
that life,
that promised life,
that promised resurrected life,
that will be yours,
after this death, and this departing.

For it will come,
and you will know the bonds of love again,
anew, afresh, at one with me once more.
Not now,
not known,
not near,
nor clear as you would want and hope,
not yet continuing on in love
and new creative ways.

But it will come,
that shaft of light from deep inside
the blackness of your sky,
will bring a promised day of hope again.

This is my plea –
begin with this death.
This is your task –
begin with this loss.
This is your beginning –
begin with this ending.
This is your step of faith –
begin with my departing.
And this is the promise you will know –
that life and love
with me,
will come for you once more.

For Davy

I never heard you sing,
And yet you sang your song to me with silent words,
When music played.

I never saw you laugh,
And yet your eyes lit up a room when people came.
You made them smile.

I never knew your style,
And yet you still drew people near to you each time
By being you.

I never was your friend,
And yet I knew, I saw, I understood a love
That never died.

I never held your hand,
And yet your eyes said all that could be said to me
Of holding on.

I never said goodbye,
And yet I know for sure you will prepare yourself
For long hellos.

I never let you go,
And yet you are not here, to sing, to laugh, to share again
With loving friends.

I never see you now,
And yet you still remain in memory's private place
For ever real.

Seven

Where is God now?

'Your God is a bastard!'
Anon: 'A need for living'

'There lives more faith in honest doubt, believe me, than in half the creeds.'
Tennyson: 'In Memoriam'

I have to confess that when *A Need for Living* was published I was surprised not to receive any adverse comments about the prayer at the end of one of the chapters which contained the above quote from one of our grieving relatives. I suppose the puritanical, Presbyterian part of me was concerned with choosing to put a swear-word in print, even though it was a direct quotation from someone else! The Christian part of me wondered, too, if it was OK to put such a dramatic condemnation of God on paper, even though the passion and vehemence of the comment were very real and valid, and even though the devastation behind the vehemence was something with which I could clearly identify.

The lack of overt criticism of the choice to use such language suggests that even for those who blanch at such vehemence, especially against God, and are appalled at the use of foul swear-words, the depth of pain that created such an outburst gives it its validity. For even mild-mannered people get angry sometimes. And even Christians have doubts, though they often remain hidden, and there is, thankfully, a recognition of their importance when they are expressed by someone else. So, 'Your God is a bastard' represents something very important, the bursting forth of anger at God, and a railing against an apparently loving God at the injustice of a death.

So it was with Bill. A church elder, and a fine, upstanding man; a role model, if ever there was one, of fortitude, of stability and of faith; a veritable paragon of service, of commitment, and of obedience to God ... all, indeed, that one would expect to be in the job-description of a man of God and a 'pillar of the Kirk'. Yet this was the man who in my hearing, after the funeral service of his twin brother who had been killed in a tragic accident, exclaimed with anger and doubt: 'Where is God now? Where is this God who promised me strength? Where is my "blessed assurance" that all will be well? Where is the "triumph o'er the grave"? Where is God now?'

Why should I expect not to feel the same thing from time to time? It is OK to be 'out of control' as I was when Talbot died, even though it did not feel so at the time. And why should other people not expect to feel the same? Yet they struggle for a validation of their real feelings – because they have to be strong and a witness for their faith; because they are uncomfortable with doubt; because they don't want to let God down. So their doubts, their anger, their railing at God, their real and honest feelings are so often suppressed, and, as a result, the bereavement journey is all the more difficult and tortuous.

Geoff Walters in his excellent book *Why Do Christians Find it Hard to Grieve?*[31] explores some of the theological reasons for this. One facet is the corruption of Gospel theology with the absorption of the Greek concept of the immortality of the soul. If life continues in immortality, and we are only separated from our loved ones by the thin veil of death, and if therefore our faith tells us that they are safe and happy and we will be reunited with them some day, why should we be unhappy for them, and why should we grieve in our loss? Yet the human emotions of grief – the sorrow and pain and devastation – are real, even for those who have a faith perspective. Better, says Walters, to return to Gospel theology, of life and death and resurrection, to live for a time in the tomb of death before any resurrection, any beginning again, can be possible, in this world or in any world to come.

Not many people nowadays are familiar with Greek or Gospel concepts. So I often point to the words of the Psalmist, for here I find someone who is real, and a journey of faith that wrestles with all the realities of living. The same Psalmist who can say in Psalm 23, 'Even though I walk through the valley of the shadow of death, I will fear no evil … Goodness and mercy will follow me all the days of my life, and I will live in the house of the Lord for ever' one of the great affirmations of faith sung so regularly at funerals in its metrical form – can also say with passion in Psalm 22, 'My God, my God, why have you forsaken me?' – the words of Jesus himself on the cross.

As with the book of Lamentations from which I quoted earlier, I like the book of Psalms because it is about real emotions. The writer of the psalms is a real person giving expression to real situations on behalf of real people. So you find contained within the one hundred and fifty psalms the whole spectrum of human feeling and the whole range of attitudes towards God.

For example, Psalm 6: 'Don't punish me in your anger' and 'How long, O Lord, will you wait to help me?' How often have I heard both of these sentiments from grieving people, as they equate the pain of suffering and death with the punishment of God, and as they seek strength from the God they believe in and find none? In Psalm 13: 'How much longer will you hide yourself from me?' 'Restore my strength, don't let me die' – as the spectre of death is seen as the ultimate defeat of love and faith. In Psalm 44: in which the Psalmist recalls what the community used to believe about God, complains that they are now afflicted by a crisis they did nothing to deserve, and in the end pleads with God to stir himself: 'Wake up, Lord! Why are you asleep? Rouse yourself! Don't reject us for ever. Why are you hiding from us? Don't forget our suffering and trouble.' – when faith has departed and God appears to have abandoned his loving people. It is no wonder that Robert Davidson, former professor of Old Testament in Glasgow University, pointed out in a seminar in our hospice recently that there are more 'whys' and 'how longs' in the Psalms than there are hallelujahs!

But, then again, like Gospel and Greek concepts, not many people nowadays are familiar with the psalms either. So, I tell them stories. Like the one that was told to me by Bob. Bob was my father's age and was a youth worker when I was a teenager. He was happily married, and had two sons, of whom he was justifiably proud. He was a church elder, a good Christian man, and an excellent role-model for young people like me. Tragically, one of his sons was killed in a motorcycle accident. The family were devastated, and Bob was a broken man. I knew little of this at the time, for I was too young to understand and was not directly involved then with the family anyway. But when Bob and I got to know each other again in adult life as our paths crossed professionally we were able to talk a little about the events of his son's death. And he told me a story which, he said, was the single most important thing that had kept him going through it all.

He had read in a book an account of a man whose daughter had acute myeloid leukaemia. This devastating cancer of the blood is severely life-limiting, and the chances of surviving it are not good. However, the staff in the hospital where his daughter was being cared for were wonderful. The chaplain was available. Treatments were offered. Support was given. Hopes were kept alive. And every day he visited his daughter. And, being a devout Christian, every day he visited the hospital chapel on his way in to the ward. And every day he knelt before the altar. And every day he prayed for a miracle. And every day he had faith in God.

On the day of his daughter's birthday, he bought her a birthday cake to share the celebration with her in the hospital, and took it up to the ward. On his way, he went to the chapel as usual, knelt at the altar-rail, and prayed. When he got to the ward the screens were round his daughter's bed. As he got closer, the screens parted and a doctor and nurse emerged. He could tell by the look on their faces that his daughter had died. No one needed to say anything. He turned on his heel, went back to the hospital chapel, took the cake, raised it above his head, and stuck it in the face of the crucifix. Such was his pain that at that moment God was a bastard, and got the full force of his anger. 'Where is God now?' Such an expression of honesty, Bob told me, such an expression of doubt, vehemence and devastation, had been enormously helpful to him, and began to give him permission to be honest about his own brokenness and anger and doubt in the very existence of a loving God. So he read and reread that story. For, he said, it was the only thing that made any sense.

I worked some years ago with Andrew, an elderly man whose faith community for seventy years had been the Plymouth Brethren. We talked at length of faith and obedience to God. He knew the Bible better than I did – and told me so! But I also knew from the nursing staff that Andrew was very frightened, that he could not settle at night, that he was fearful of closing his eyes in case he didn't waken up. I talked with him about this one morning. He told me that it was true, that he was indeed frightened, but that this was obviously because he didn't have enough faith. If he did, he wouldn't be frightened. So he would pray more, read the Bible more, almost flagellate himself for his 'unbelief' in the hope that it would take the fear away. It never did. And Andrew died a very restless and anxious man.

Fear is not the antithesis of faith; the two walk hand in hand. Doubt and anger are not the opposites of belief; they are integral to it. Human emotions are not a diminution of a commitment to your God; they are part of what we are as God's people. So Bill's reaction, and Bob's, and the man's in Bob's story, and the Psalmist's, and our Lord's, were right. That is what God expects, if you like – a God who can stand the heat, who can take the blows, and waits for you to calm down! 'God is big enough to take our anger …'

That is why I took the risk one evening of being honest with John. A young man of twenty-three, John was suffering from the same leukaemia which had affected the young woman in Bob's story. John was a qualified accountant, having come top in his year. He was a keen sportsman, and a ruggedly handsome individual. Again, well supported by good people, family, friends and professionals, John was coping with his dying journey with enormous dignity. He was a lovely man, and that made his dying for all who came into contact with him very hard indeed. I'm not ashamed to tell you that I shed a few tears in my dealings with John, and I suspect many of his other carers did too.

Early one evening I slipped in to see John before I went home. He'd had a bad day, he looked pale and drawn, and things were obviously deteriorating for him. I was tired too, and, to be honest, I had only slipped in for a few moments so that I had 'done my duty', so to speak, at the end of the day. John looked anxious, not afraid, but just anxious. He took my hand and looked me straight in the eye. It was obvious to me that he wanted me to offer him something, some words of comfort, anything that would make sense of this. But I had nothing to say. I was as anxious as he was – and I suspect he saw that in my eyes too. We looked at each other for what seemed an age. And then I whispered, 'John, this is hellish.' There was a long pause, and then he smiled and said, 'You're not supposed to say that.' 'I'm sorry for the language,' I said. 'No, not the language. But you're not supposed to say this is hellish. You're supposed to offer some hope, give some reason, share some explanation.' 'I don't have any hope to offer you,' I said, 'I see no reason in this, no explanation that makes it right. Right at this moment I just feel the hellishness of it all. That's all I can say.' There was a long pause. 'You're the only one that's said that,' John said eventually. 'You're the only one who's said what's true.' After a while we parted, and a few days later John was dead. Did he find peace in the face of death? I don't actually know. But had he been offered a chance to be real with his feelings, and to be honest about his faith? I hope so.

It is not destructive to acknowledge or to articulate the hellishness of the journey of dying or bereavement. It is, I believe, the beginning of healing, the starting point of an honest reformation of belief and a faith perspective. It is not destructive to feel the hellishness of those who weep and be unable to offer trite words or cheap sympathy. Nor is it failure. For the gift of being at one with those who mourn is to begin to create a context in which acceptance and understanding can be the forerunners of wholeness.

I have often sensed in the writings of other people that, in being able to express their struggles with the human condition, they actually understand my own grief and sorrow. Why? Because the way they write about their experiences resonates with my own life. Such is the gift and the beauty of good poetry, for example. One such poem comes from the pen of Samuel Johnson, and reflects on the death of one Dr Robert Levet[32]. I do not know the significance of Dr Levet either to Johnson or to anyone else. I do not know whether Johnson is expressing his own grief or the sorrow that is being experienced by Dr Levet's family and friends on his death. But I do know, in the depth of his expressive words, that Johnson understands me, and that Robert Levet, therefore, stands for all those people for whom I have grieved and grieve now. The poem contains these verses:

When fainting nature call'd for aid,
And hovering death prepar'd the blow,
His vig'rous remedy display'd
The power of art without the show.

In misery's darkest caverns known,
His useful care was ever nigh,
Where hopeless anguish pour'd his groan,
And lonely want retir'd to die.

Grief drags us into the darkest of caverns, those lightless caves which are filled with fear and devoid of God. Loss brings to us unfathomable misery, at times overwhelming and without hope. Bereavement pours anguish upon us, and we take up the groans of countless people before us. Sorrow brings us a loneliness from which the only escape may seem death itself. And yet I believe, and I have seen it in those who are broken by grief and I have known it to be true for those who offer their faltering and reluctant compassion, that, in the most mysterious of paradoxes, it is the very acceptance of that hopelessness, the very expression of it, that is the beginning of the return of hope.

In the midst of the search for meaning which is common to us all as we wrestle with the big questions of living and dying, there are some who work out their own meaning in religious terms. Creeds, belief systems, religious symbols, corporate acts of worship and sacraments mean a lot, and give a framework for the search for hope and purpose. If, however, religion creates such a straightjacket of belief that it denies true feelings, then, instead of being a liberation and a support, it becomes an oppression and a tyranny. That, I feel, was where Andrew was. True religion should have room within it for true feelings. Real beliefs in God should carry within them real doubts and uncertainties.

In his book *Courage to Doubt*[33], Bob Davidson explores this recurrent theme from the Old Testament, and concludes with this reflection:

Calmness and self confidence are not the words that naturally spring to mind when we think of Jeremiah or Job or many of the psalms of lament. It is the struggle to maintain certainties in the midst of uncertainty, in the painful groping for new light in the midst of a darkness that seems total, that the Old Testament bears its clearest witness to the courage to doubt.

I believe Tennyson when he writes[34] *'There lives more faith in honest doubt, believe me, than in half the creeds.'* The courage to doubt, not to know and to say so, are, or should be, integral to our beliefs. And if that is so, why should they not be integral to the way our beliefs speak to our journeys of loss?

I have written in an earlier chapter of being out of control in the face of grief. Such an expression of the devastation of loss comes from deep within us, and is fundamentally an anger, a raging, at what has happened. In a dignified but nonetheless heartfelt way, Glenda in the opening chapter was expressing such anger, directed at the husband who had abandoned her with so many promises unfulfilled. And in a later chapter I'll return to the theme of anger as an expression of grief in this and other ways. But, in the context of this chapter, are we not expressing our anger at God, the God in whom we have believed, in whose love we have felt secure, and who has now done the dirty on us by failing to protect us from the pain and devastation of death and the torture of our feelings of grief?

I do not believe that it is always wrong to be angry or that anger is the enemy of love. Nor do I believe that it is always wrong to be angry with our God or that this anger is the enemy of faith. Of course anger can be destructive and many people will say they have lost their faith in the face of tragedy. But there are other ways, alternatives to the destructive forces of our anger at God, which can lead to personal, social and religious liberation.

These are themes which Alastair Campbell explores with insight and depth in his book *The Gospel of Anger*[35] – a book which should be essential reading for any religious practitioner or follower of a belief system whose religious framework tyrannises them and denies them the right to be in touch with real feelings. For so often our doubts and anger remain far from validated, and we are made to feel they are the antithesis of faith. Alastair Campbell writes: 'In the bleak times of overwhelming grief, anger may seem just an additional agony. It can be so. Anger, literally in the gut causing nausea and pain, anger bringing clenched fists and tense shoulders, anger causing restless and useless movement, a lashing out at things or a pacing up and down, anger adding hot discomfort and a choking feeling to the wet defencelessness of tears – all these bodily reactions fuel the sense of helplessness and loss of control which grieving often creates. But, like weeping, anger has an important part to play in the healing of the wounds of loss.'

Alastair Campbell is right. Anger does have an important part to play in the healing of the wounds of loss. But I would go further. For I believe that anger also has an important part to play in the healing of the wounds of faith.

When Michael lost his mother he was devastated. He and his mother had been best friends as well as mother and son, having been brought ever closer in the years following the sudden death of his father when Michael was in his teens. And now, in his thirties, never having left home, he had to face life without his mother after he had lost her to cancer some months before. He knew that he had become dependent on his mother as she had, indeed, become dependent on her son. And that mutual dependence, perhaps looked on as unhealthy by outsiders, was the sustaining force for both of them as the years had gone by. But there was more. For religion played an important part in both their lives too. Their regular attendance at Mass, the healing effect of their Catholic faith, the sustaining of their beliefs and their shared expression of it, was crucial to their lives. Michael and his mother were at Mass every Sunday. They never missed Confession or a Saint's Day. Their faith was so important. God was good. And, indeed, so it continued through Michael's mother's dying. The priest was a regular visitor. The Sacraments, the offices of his religion, were offered and openly welcomed. The Requiem Mass for the funeral was a great occasion of faith and cele-bration. The priest was supportive and attentive. God was good.

So it was ... until some months after the funeral. Michael had been aware of an increasingly empty feeling as he attended worship, and an increasing anger at the apparent emptiness of the words of the Mass. Indeed, he even began to feel an antithesis towards the priest, a resentment at his certainty and the strength of the faith he represented. Over the weeks, though he never missed a Sunday, Michael was aware that he was withdrawing from any meaning there had ever been for him in going to Mass, or, perhaps, the meaning of it all was withdrawing from him. And he knew that he was getting angry with God.

But why? Wasn't God good? Wasn't his mother safe in God's hands? Wasn't doubt sinful? Wouldn't anger have to be confessed to and a sinner have to do penance? Such was his turmoil. And such was his confusion as he slipped into the chapel one weekday evening. For a time he knelt quietly in a pew as he'd often done. But this time, there was more. Tears began to run down his face. His fists were clenched and his knuckles were white. He began to bang his hands on the pew in front. He was raging with anger inside, and it was getting out of control. He knew he should leave before he did damage to himself or to something else. But he didn't.

Before he knew what he was doing, he had risen from his feet and moved towards one of the side chapels. Then he had taken a small plaster statue of the Madonna and Child from an alcove at the side. And, lifting it high above his head, he had brought in crashing down on the altar rail, smashing it into a thousand pieces. And he cursed God. He cursed the goodness of God. He cursed the love of God. He cursed the existence of God. And he lay and wept on the altar steps amid the fragments of the shattered Madonna, amidst the ruins of a shattered faith. It may have been for moments or hours. He had no consciousness of the passing of time. He had no idea if anyone had even seen him there. If they had, no one had come to intrude on his private devastation. But when he began to focus again, he had a strange sense of inner peace. He rose to his feet and left the sanctuary, leaving behind him the shattered remains of his angry outburst.

Michael went back to Mass the following Sunday, and still goes every week. There's a new Madonna and Child in the side-chapel alcove, and the destruction of the original one has never been mentioned, at least not to him. There's a chip in the altar rail that's never been repaired. Maybe no one knows it's there, but Michael does. He tells me he still gets angry with God, though he doesn't smash plaster statues any more.

Alistair Campbell tells us, 'It seems, then, that the deeper we penetrate into the mystery of God, the less we understand rationally why faith endures ... And yet, in knowing God in mystery, even in dread and despair, we know our true self as that which suffers and so as that which loves. There was no answer to [the suffering and complaints of] Job – but in his angry questioning he met his God.'

So too, in his angry questioning, in his destruction of the Madonna and Child, symbolic, perhaps, of the destruction of his meek-and-mild, accepting-and-never-questioning faith, it would seem that Michael met his God again. And maybe this is a God who is more real, more true, and, who knows, a God of whom Michael can still say, 'God is good.'

Notes

31 *Why Do Christians Find it Hard to Grieve?*, by Geoff Walters, published by Paternoster Press, Carlisle, 1997.
32 Samuel Johnson (1709–1784), from 'On the Death of Dr Robert Levet'.
33 *Courage to Doubt* by Robert Davidson; published by SCM Press, 1983, ISBN 334 01957 5; reprinted with permission.
34 Alfred Lord Tennyson, from 'In memoriam'.
35 *The Gospel of Anger* by Alastair V. Campbell, published by SPCK, 1986, ISBN 0 281 04221 7.

I look for you

I look for you
in practised ritual,
for often I had known you there.
But now the ritual rings
with hollow sounds
of emptiness,
and speaks to me of falseness
and of broken promises.

I look for you
in holy words,
for there
you had revealed your truth.
But now the words are all confused.
Like newly painted water-colours
in a gentle rain,
the cherished picture is no more.
You have no form or colour now.

I look for you
in shaded walks
and secret haunts
where once we dwell in harmony.
But now the paths are overgrown
and special places feel
no more like home.
You do not come as once you did.
And now I wait,
and watch,
and walk in vain.

I look for you
in trust of those I most admire,
to whom I turn
to feed upon their faith.
But if they looked upon me once,
they turn away,
embarrassed now
by doubts and fears
no longer hid
from this, my searching gaze.

I look for you
in endless sighs
of silent hours,
and moments
which are days of emptiness.
But holy silence now becomes
oppressive shouts of nothingness,
and nothingness
speaks louder now
than hope.

I look for you
in rising sun
and evening rain,
in springtime's hope
and autumn's fading sheen.
But no,
not even there,
as month will follow month
do you reveal yourself again,
surprising me
in nature's changing scenes.

I look,
and look again,
I hope and dream.
I do expect,
believe,
have faith.
But no,
no sight,
no sound,
no fleeting glance,
no whispered breath,
no joy from expectation's risk,
no echo from my call of faith.

I look,
and look again.
I hope and dream.
But hope
in fading understanding,
And dream
in fruitless faith.

She came to me

She came to me,
a nurse whom I had known
   in her efficient tenderness
   and loving care,
   for me –
this vigil-keeper,
   this faithful watcher by a dying frame.

She came to me,
to offer once again
   her tender efficiency
   and deep concern
   to me
this adult child
   now growing into grief.

She came to me –
but did she know
   what now I had become,
   this useless thing,
   this me,
this faithless doubter,
   far removed from God?

She came to me
and touched my hand,
   then held me in a soft embrace
   of tenderness,
   held me,
this frightened, lonely child
   in search of God.

She came to me,
and held my grieving soul
    in safe and tender hands
    of love
    for me,
and all I had become
    now he had gone.

She came to me,
this nurse, whom now I knew
    for what she had become,
    a lover of this broken soul.
    And me?
I sensed the Love of this embrace
    now holding me.

She came to me,
shedding her efficiency and tears,
    yet offering not a word
    that might intrude upon a silence which,
    for me,
Said God was there
    in love, and silent tears.

That moment

That moment of your smile,
Was that the smile of God?

That moment of your touch,
Was that God's tender hand?

That moment of your warmth,
Was that God's warm embrace?

That moment of your truth,
Was that God's wisdom shown?

That moment of your peace,
Was that God's peace for me?

That moment of your death,
Was that God's time for you?

That moment of my doubt,
Was God's acceptance there?

That moment of my faith,
Was that God's gift to me?

That moment of my joy,
Was that God's hopeful sign?

That moment of my tears,
Was that my God come close?

That moment, still and deep,
Was that the voice of God?

Eight

Impossible expectations of coping

'Blessed is the man whose strength is in thee: in whose heart are thy ways. Who going through the vale of misery, use it for a well: and the pools are filled with water. They will go from strength to strength.'
The 1662 Prayer Book

'This is impossible for man, but for God everything is possible.'
Bible: Matthew 19:26

I have long been of the opinion that we cannot fully understand bereavement unless we have personal experiences through which to filter changing theories of grief and loss and the stories that are told by other people of their own journey. We can offer sympathy, and indeed compassion and consolation can give tremendous healing support to those who struggle with the processes of grief. A kind word, a listening ear, a caring attitude, a sensitive touch, a supportive action, all have their place in communicating to bereaved people that they have not been abandoned by the rest of the world.

I know that in the early years of my ministry I was, to be honest, very short of meaningful personal experiences to draw upon. But I hope I was able to minister with compassion to those who had lost a loved one, where a funeral had to be arranged, and a platform of support established from which the bereaved could step off into an unknown future. I do hope so. Yet, however good one might be in this sympathetic role, however much compassion and consolation we show to comfort and support bereaved people, I am absolutely sure that we cannot really understand what they are going through unless we have worked through the pain and feelings of loss in our own journey.

That is not to say that knowledge of theory is unimportant. Too many people – and in this, sadly, I include some professionals to whom people turn in their time of need – have either a scant understanding of grief theory or have based their practice on theories which, though they were useful in their time, have been superseded by more contemporary and, I believe, more workable concepts. This is not a theoretical book, so if people wish to explore current thinking on grief and loss they will have to look elsewhere. But to put it simply, what might be called 'traditional' theories of grief, which place a bereaved person in definable and time-limited stages, do not fit my own reality of bereavement work. Indeed, we were informed by one widower in our bereavement support groups that his psychiatrist had told him he was stuck at the first stage of grief (whatever that is). And it seemed to us that, having been so labelled, he deemed this sufficient to define and justify his unwillingness to work at his loss and move on from the death of his wife. Current theories, on the other hand, talk more helpfully of the work that is required in the grief process, and the developing, over time, of a continuing relationship with the person who has died. The work of the ongoing grief journey includes a process of reforming our relationships.

These ideas are most helpfully outlined in *Continuing Bonds*, edited by Dennis Klass, Phyllis Silverman and Steven Nickman[36]. Not surprisingly, the subtitle of their book is 'New understandings of grief'. In their preface the editors write: 'The continuing bond has been overlooked or undervalued … Grief goes further than the fact that people maintain a relationship to the deceased person … It requires that we look at the way we see relationships in general in our society. We need to bring into our professional dialogue the reality of how people experience and live their lives, rather than finding ways of verifying preconceived theories of how people should live.'

People deal intuitively with loss. Mostly they don't know they're doing it, and they have no real idea how they cope. But they do what they do. They work to maintain a relationship with the deceased person, to keep it going, not wanting to lose what has been so good and right. And they learn to adjust to a new shape for that relationship over time, and to be comfortable with that. It is a sad fact that it is often only in bereavement that people begin to examine and talk about what love really means and the nature of the relationship that has preceded the loss. As the bereavement journey unfolds, it can give a positive affirmation of the continuing and unfolding nature of our relationships, but it also gives the opportunity to look at the nature of these relationships in the first place.

I worked with one widow in her later years who was labelled by her doctor as exhibiting signs of denying the loss of her husband and being unwilling to move on from it because she still kept his toothbrush beside hers in the bathroom. She told me she kept the toothbrush there not only because it had always been there, but also because, first thing in the morning, it reminded her of her husband. Of course she knew her husband was dead. She wasn't hanging on to him in any way or denying he was gone. She was simply holding on to those things, a toothbrush included, that helped her remember what it had been like when her husband was around.

Our bereavement support team supported a younger widow who had been instructed by her Community Psychiatric Nurse to show that she was moving on in her grief by packing up all the things that reminded her of her husband, his clothes and the like, and storing them in the attic. It was considered 'unhealthy' not to have sorted these things out. And she told us she was made to feel worse and not better by this additional pressure. With both of these women, it was clear that limited theoretical frameworks were being used and imposed which succeeded in narrowing an understanding of loss, rather that creating the openness which was more necessary and appropriate.

When the widow explained that she kept her husband's tooth-brush beside hers because that's where it had always been, and when the young woman cried when she said she felt that putting her husband's clothes in the attic was like shutting him away, then their way of coping should have been affirmed for what it was, an attempt to adjust to a new way of relating, an unfolding of their continuing bond with the person who had died. In our approach to grief and loss, we need to understand the reality of how people experience and live their lives, rather than find ways of verifying preconceived notions of how they should live and journey through their bereavement.

Alongside this, we must also remember that one kind of loss cannot give insight into every other kind of loss which people experience. It can give clues. It can help with an understanding and acceptance of feelings and reactions. It can create in us a feeling of empathy. But it cannot and should not give all the answers. While I work, for example, with many people who are struggling to cope with the loss of a partner, I cannot ever say, 'I understand how you feel,' to such people, for I have not, thank God, had to face the pain of the death of my wife. Of course, I can gain insight into such a loss from my knowledge of other losses. And, even more, I can draw upon my years of experience of working with those who have actually lost a partner. But the distinctive nature of the loss of a husband, wife or partner remains beyond my personal experience and understanding.

So, current theories are important, and we need to be aware of the limitations of our understanding when we extrapolate from one loss to every loss. But it is still crucially important to recognise that personal experience of loss at any level, and the processes of dealing with such a loss, are essential ingredients in any offering of help and understanding to people who are bereaved. Self-knowledge is important if one is to try with any degree of confidence to enter into the painful world which the bereaved are forced to inhabit.

As a consequence, as well as reflecting on the deaths of close friends, I am called often to reflect on and learn from the deaths of the two people in my life which have had the biggest impact on me. These reflections, and the lessons learned from them, are not 'one-off' events as you will see, but have created for me an ongoing opportunity over many years and in a variety of ways to learn and grow.

My mother died when I was in my early thirties. She had had a heart condition for several years, but died unexpectedly at the age of fifty-eight following a relatively routine operation for a replacement heart valve. I hadn't had to cope with the death of someone close to me before. I hadn't had what someone called recently 'the practice run' of the loss of grandparents I had known and liked. My father's parents had died when he was young, so I never knew them. My mother's father had died ten years or so before, but I was never really close to him, so his death and his funeral were more something to be observed and reflected on than to be felt and grieved over. He was outlived by my granny for many years, and, indeed, for some time after my mother died. But with my mother it was different. This was my mother, a woman who was the epitome of goodness, and the major influence on my faith journey. She was no saint, and we argued a lot – she was menopausal when I was in my rebellious teens, a challenge to sainthood for sure! – but I admired and loved her greatly and she was proud of me, my calling and my family.

Following the operation, my mother lay in a coma for five days. At the end, I recall my wife coming to find me in the parish to tell me the hospital had called and I'd better get there right away. I remember nothing else till I was standing with my father beside my mother's bed. I remember after she died a young doctor struggling to ask if they could use my mother's corneas for transplant purposes, and me and my dad making the asking easy for him, so pleased were we that a death could bring some healing to someone else. I remember wanting to relieve my dad's stress and sadness as he phoned round family and friends to tell them what had happened. And I remember little else, until, nearly a week after the death, we were all together in the family home waiting for the funeral to happen.

I remember choosing not to cry. I remember standing at the graveside and comforting my dad, my sister, my granny and my wife. And, above all, I remember feeling that I had to be strong. I was a man, a son, a husband, a brother, a father, a grandson, and a minister. Whatever was happening to me – and though not crying was a conscious choice I suspect that I had little control over anything else that was going on – all of these roles were informing my behaviour at that time. And they were telling me that I had to cope for the rest of the people, for if I didn't, who were they going to rely on then? I could feel myself burdened by expectations, but I was powerless to do anything about it. What might be possible for God was clearly 'impossible for man'[37] – and for this man in particular. Even if I'd had enough insight to know what was happening, I would still have had little control over what I was and how I was reacting and the roles I was obliged to fulfil.

How often men feel that in the face of grief they should take on the mantle of strength, and, especially in stoical Western society, deem it unacceptable, and indeed see it is a sign of weakness, to cry in public. I heard an interesting insight from a minister colleague recently. He was reflecting on the day when he and many others were devastated in the extreme when Heart of Midlothian Football Club had the anticipated Scottish Premier League Championship snatched from their grasp on the very last day of the season. He recalled sitting on the terracing steps and weeping, devastated at the tragedy which had befallen his beloved Hearts, and looking around and seeing dozens, perhaps hundreds, of grown men openly crying, holding each other and sharing tears together, such was the depth of their sorrow. Take the same men, he suggested, to a church funeral or to the local crematorium, to the devastation of the death of a colleague, a friend, a brother or a son, and the absence of tears and a public expression of the grief of a loss would be equally obvious.

It was no different for me. If I cried, I cried alone, and, as I recall, I did little enough even of that. For the public persona, the 'me' I deemed it fit to present in the public context, was about control, strength and stoicism. I had no other model to follow. Acting in that way was all I knew. And there was the Christian bit too, the obedience to God bit, the witnessing to the world bit, the 'Blessed is the man whose strength is in thee' bit, whose faith means that he will, or should, go 'from strength to strength'. Was this not what faith was about? Was my mother not safe in God's hands? Was God not a good God who would give us the strength we needed, for whom 'everything was possible'? Was I not his servant who had to be strong as a witness to my faith? Was I not a minister who always had to be a shining example to others? Oh, I can understand all of that now and can view my reactions through the excellent twin lenses of hindsight and life-experience. But then ... what did I know? I was what I was. I coped as I had to cope. I fulfilled the roles I had no choice but to fulfil. I acted the part with commitment.

The problem of fulfilling these roles was further compounded when I came back to work in my parish after the events of the funeral and its aftermath were over. I had no sooner arrived back in the manse than I was contacted by a church family to say that their old granny was dying, and could I come round. Granny Robertson was one of my favourite people, a feisty, honest, caring woman with whom I had a super relationship. 'She hung on till you got back, you know,' I was told. And I could feel my return to minister-role begin at that very point. Granny Robertson died peacefully while I sat by her bedside, so she may well have waited on my return. But with that, and the comfort offered to the family, and preparing the funeral, and a full crematorium singing Granny Robertson's favourite hymn[38], I was right back in full swing.

Come, children, join to sing –
Alleluia! Amen!
Loud praise to Christ our King;
Alleluia! Amen!
Let all, with heart and voice,
Before His throne rejoice;
Praise is His greatest choice:
Alleluia! Amen!

Come, lift your hearts on high;
Alleluia! Amen!
Let praises fill the sky;
Alleluia! Amen!
He is our Guide and Friend;
To us He'll blessing send;
His love shall never end:
Alleluia! Amen!

Praise yet the Lord again;
Alleluia! Amen!
Life shall not end the strain;
Alleluia! Amen!
On heaven's blissful shore
His goodness we'll adore,
Singing for evermore.
Alleluia! Amen!

Wonderful stuff! That's what it was all about. Faith to be affirmed, praises to be sung, God to be thanked. And with that especially powerful affirmation of the final verse, I was right back in role – the coper, the strong one, the minister to be leaned on, the unshakeable rock to serve as an anchor for others.

It wasn't until some years later that I revisited all of that through counselling (and how hard that was when at last I realised that I had to find out where my destructive work-patterns were coming from before it was too late and I did damage to myself with over-work). During the counselling process I was enabled to see what had been happening. Could I have handled my mother's death and its aftermath any differently at the time? I doubt it. 'This is impossible for man.' I reacted, as I suspect most of us do, in the only way I could. I was a victim of forces beyond my control and understanding at that stage in my life. The mantle which had fallen on me was one which I now know gave me impossible expectations of coping, expectations which almost forced me to pay the ultimate price.

Twenty years later, when my father suffered a stroke at the age of eighty, things were very different. Self-knowledge, counselling, life-experience, other losses worked through in a more constructive and healthy fashion, had all begun to inform me in a different way. Three months' sabbatical leave in the remarkable 'Church of the Saviour' in Washington DC in 1989 had been the catalyst for all of that. And now I stood by my dad's bedside as he struggled for words, and I knew I was staring his death in the face. He asked for my sister and for my wife. He spoke the names of my three children. I knew what he was doing. He was surrounding himself with the love of his family members because he thought he was going to die.

Thankfully, he survived that stroke, and, though greatly incapacitated and living a very different kind of life from that which he had known before, he went on living with my sister for another year and a half. Did he tell me he thought he was going to die when he was in his hospital bed? Not a chance, for being open about feelings was never part of the loving relationship we had. He never gave up on life, never talked about death, never opened up on any of the things he might have needed to sort or finish. He just lived till he died. But living with his dying was now very different for me, very different from the experiences around the death of my mother. Why? Because

I was now a different person. It's not just that I'd become more comfortable with tears, and that my work in the hospice had taught me such a lot about real feelings and how death could be handled. It's simply that somewhere along the way I'd been able to ditch the 'impossible expectations of coping'. The me of now was a different and more healthy me than I had known before.

The last few months of my dad's life were a real struggle. My wife and I would travel north after work on a Friday every third weekend or so and look after my dad till the Sunday evening to allow my sister to get a break. My sister, Margaret, had been wonderful through all of this, but it was beginning to wear her down. And I could see why, for caring for my dad, even for a couple of days, was extraordinarily stressful.

In time, my dad moved into a local nursing home where he spent the last few weeks of his life. My wife and I still went up as often as we could, every second weekend or so. By now I knew that death wasn't far away. I had to light his cigarette for him and hold it in his mouth. I would try to draw him into conversation by talking with him about some of the routes he used to travel in his bus-driving days. Towards the end, there was very little recognition of anything at all. And every time I left the home after seeing him I found myself sitting on the little wall by the front door and crying for my loss. In a sense I was telling myself every time it was the last time I was going to see him. And, eventually, it was.

When the call came to say he'd died peacefully in his sleep, I was ready. The funeral, the business affairs, the loss, were all tackled very differently from the way I had reacted to the death of my mother. Tears were OK. I didn't need to be responsible for anyone else. Even ministers cry, for goodness' sake! But this time I wasn't the minister, I wasn't the image, I wasn't the role. I was, instead, a grieving son of a father who had died. That was the primary role which it was necessary to fulfil. I remember saying to my colleagues much later that I felt like two different people – the professional, who knew about such things as grief and loss, and the grieving son who mourned for his dad – and that sometimes these two people were a long way apart, with nothing to say to each other. Looking back, that feels good and right, for it meant I was what I needed to be, someone learning to cope with the death of a father for myself.

So, I grieved for the loss, and now, quite healthily, I grieve for the loss of both my parents. For at the age of fifty, I was orphaned, and that didn't feel awfully great, I can tell you. But the difference in the way I reacted to those two deaths twenty years apart was informed by a lifetime of learning and growing, which – if it's anything at all to do with God – is more of what I now believe the 'going from strength to strength' in the 1662 prayer book[39] is all about.

I now feel that I have continuing bonds with both of my parents. I am clearer about the bond with my mother in working through the death of my father, and clearer too about the nature of the relationships and the love we shared, in life and in death. I had recognised the impossible expectations of coping too, and as a result have begun to cope better than I could ever have expected.

The week I got back to the hospice after my dad's funeral, I realised that getting back to work was harder than I had anticipated. I had decided to have nothing to do with bereavement support work for a while that was never in doubt – but I wasn't ready for the tiredness and the feeling of walking through treacle that the loss had brought with it. So I mostly kept out of people's way and got on with my job. After a day or so, I was sitting at the desk in one of the nursing duty-rooms writing some notes when a staff nurse, who didn't realise I was now back at work, came in. 'Oh, Tom, good to see you back. How are you?' 'Fine. I'm OK,' I replied without lifting my head from the notes. The nurse quietly closed the door and said, 'How are you really?' Tears welled up in my eyes. 'I'm OK,' I whispered. 'No … I'm not really … But I will be … Thanks for asking.' And, with a hand on my shoulder, she was gone. I don't know if that nurse will remember that. But I do. And I remember how good it was to be asked how I really was. And I remember how right it was to cry.

A widow we'd worked with for a while was in one of our bereavement groups and I asked her how she was: 'Good days and bad days?' I enquired. 'No,' she replied firmly, 'not good days and bad days. Just days and bad days. There aren't any good days yet. There may not be any for a while. There may never be any ever again, I don't know. So there are days and bad days – days when I get by, and days that are unbearably hellish. So I tell people the truth – I have days and bad days, because that's how I really feel.' Impossible expectations of coping? Not for her, and not for me – not any more.

Throughout our lives we learn to wear masks, 'personae' the psychologists call them, which allow us to portray what we need to be in any given situation. I might be struggling to conduct a funeral service of someone I've known and loved, but, for a time at least, I have to wear the mask of the professional, the person who copes, who is out-front, who does what needs to be done. And that's fine, provided I can remove that mask later, and wear another one, and be the real me, the me of sadness and loss. I'm not ashamed to admit that there have been times when I have slipped round the side of the crematorium after a funeral service and cried my own tears. We have to know our masks and come to understand when it is right to wear them and when it's right to take them off and change them. Feeling that we have to cope gives us masks to wear. Sometimes we wear them because we need to or want to or have to or are forced to. And that's fine, as long as we know when they need to be changed.

When Ken went back to work after his wife's death, he coped fine. He had a team to work with, responsibilities to carry through, and a supportive company to which to repay loyalty. Why then, he asked me, did he cry on the bus on the way home? Why, when he had coped so well throughout the day, did he have to struggle with tears when he was away from work? Why could he not stop himself crying when he was alone? Because, I suggested, the mask had slipped, the mask of the capable employee, worn so well and with such ability at work, didn't need to be held in front of his face on the way home. This was the real man in real sorrow. This was real grief. This was what was true. This was still a grieving husband going home to an empty house.

Ken learned about masks, and, with some understanding and insight, came to learn what was right in what situation. He tells me he still cries sometimes, and sometimes he doesn't know why. But that's OK, because he knows himself better now, and he doesn't have impossible expectations of coping any more. So Ken, too, has days and bad days. Actually, he'll tell you he has some good days now too. I heard recently that he has a new relationship and may be getting engaged soon. Maybe some more good days ahead – who knows?

Notes

36 *Continuing Bonds: New understandings of grief,* edited by Klass, Silverman and Nickman, published by Taylor & Francis 1996, ISBN: 1 56032 339 6 (paperback)

37 Matthew 19:26, 'Jesus looked straight at them and said, "This is impossible for man, but for God everything is possible."'

38 Words by Christian Henry Bateman (1813–1889)

39 Prayer Book 1662, from Psalm 84:5,6

Masks

Well, God,
I've worn so many masks again today.
For that's the deal –
to play a role,
to act a part,
fulfilling expectations
of what I am
and what I have to be.

So I've looked calm and controlled.
But inside?
A maelstrom of turmoil.

I've been strong for others.
But who knows my weaknesses?

I've believed in you.
But when the mask slips,
am I really so sure?

So, God,
for now,
for this revealing time,
this is me,
whatever me I am –
and even I am not completely sure.
But this is me.
And you know that,
if it is known at all.

So, let me be me,
to rest with you a while.
Will you be you for me –
the You I need,
the accepting,
unconditional,
mysterious,
loving You for me?
No masks for now from either side –
what's real in me
and real of you,
at one –
at least for now.

The concept for this reflection is based on the phrase used by the widow I mentioned earlier. It was a concept which had an impact on me when she told me her story and which has remained with me ever since. The reflection, therefore, is my attempt to put into words what she might have been thinking at that time.

Days and bad days

'You'll have good days and bad days,' he said,
not knowing,
but with his expectation
of my journey of grief.
'No,' I replied,
with my own,
my painful knowing,
'I have days and bad days.'

There are no good days yet, my love,
no days like days gone by
when life was good,
and shared,
and hopeful too.
Just days
of getting by,
survival days
without you.

And bad days –
Oh, the bad days
of empty longings,
and private tears,
and broken heart,
and missing you.

'I have days and bad days,'
was the truth.

His expectation of this time?
Good days will come?
He did not say so.
Perhaps he did not know.

But I know all too well.
I know my loss of you.
So, for all of now,
days and bad days is my story,
this, my knowing,
this, my living,
this, my expectation,
these, my days and bad days,
and all my grief for you.

This door?

I found the door –
Thank God it stood ajar.
Was this the door?
Was this the way?
Was this the entrance through which I am called to go?

I pushed the door,
but it refused to move.
Was this the deal?
Was this enough?
Was this the space through which to squeeze and make my way?

I kicked the door
until my foot was sore.
Was this the style?
Was this the pain,
The pain of never knowing when the door would budge?

I beat the door,
and cursed my God again.
Was this the call?
Was this the voice?
Was this the unknown purpose of this God for me?

I closed the door,
and it slipped shut with ease.
Was this the truth?
Was this the end?
Was this the closure of the way I thought I'd found?

I left the door,
and walked away.
And down the hall another door stood just ajar.
Was this the door?
Was this the chance?
Was this the lesson learned about the way to go?

Another door,
another try.
Was this your door?
Was this your way?
Was this the moment when I would be sure –
My God, your way?

Nine

Healing words, healing moments

'Live all you can; it's a mistake not to. It doesn't matter what you do in particular, so long as you have your life. If you haven't had that, what have you had?'
Henry James, 'The Ambassadors'

*'We cannot measure how you heal
Or answer every sufferer's prayer'*
John L Bell and Graham Maule

Good support offered in the bereavement journey is invaluable. Abnormal grief reactions are, in my experience, very rare. But the lack of opportunity to check your reactions to loss against a background of what is understandable and acceptable is all too common. This can result in the isolation in bereavement which I explore elsewhere, and the perception of normal feelings as abnormalities because you have no one to tell you otherwise. Counselling is not always what is required. Of course counselling does have its place. But one-to-one therapeutic relationships in the context of a life crisis to be 'solved' and left behind are not what bereaved people mostly need. What they require is an acceptance of their grief journey and an opportunity to be listened to and to be understood for who they are and where they are on their journey. Above all else, bereaved people need a reassurance that there is no 'quick fix', but that, over time, and with patience and support, they will gain insights and acquire methodologies that can be utilised for years to come.

We offer bereavement support to every family that comes into contact with our hospice. The support is centred round small groups, meeting on a monthly basis on the first Monday evening and Thursday afternoon of every month. These groups change and reform depending on who has responded to our invitation, and the gender, relationships and age of the people attending. The bereavement support team look after these groups, each having a trained group leader. People are invited to attend until the first anniversary of their bereavement, and are thereafter encouraged to let go of our specific bereavement service, always with the promise of our continued availability, regular memorial events, and ongoing contact with the hospice in other ways. All of us who work in bereavement support find it challenging, tiring and wonderfully rewarding. For when you have the opportunity to see people move from disbelief to coping, from the devastation of the pain of loss to the dawning of the reality that they can actually begin to live again, how can you fail to feel good about the small part you play in that? 'Live all you can; it's a mistake not to.' wrote Henry James[40]. It is a genuine privilege to help people to do just that.

The ability to cope with tragedy is quite remarkable and the resilience of the human spirit has unfathomable depths. Everyone has the strength and capacity to cope. But most of us, for most of the time, are unaware that the resource exists. We have not needed it before. We don't know how to access it. We have seen others cope and we feel we'll never be as good as them. To enable individuals, therefore, to believe they have that deep well of resilience, to help them feel the confidence to access it, to see them draw on it and cope even better than they could have expected, is, not surprisingly, hugely rewarding. And it is in the context of that work that I have gained so many insights, as people teach me what coping is about, and leave me with memories and lessons which I can pass on to others.

Take, for example, what is right and what is wrong in the journey of loss, what is appropriate and what is not. How are we going to know unless we have the chance to share it with other people? And where, if we're honest, do we have the chance to be really open about how we feel anyway? Do we talk about the meaning of life and death or how we are coping with loss during the commercial break in 'Coronation Street' or over a pint with the lads in our local? I suspect not!

I had a group of three men to work with one evening, all in their sixties, and all struggling with the reality of coping without their life-partner. Two had been to our groups before – Tommy bereaved for six months or so and George about eight months – and one man, Jim, was attending for the first time, his wife having died in our hospice about ten weeks previously. They were open and supportive of each other, though Jim took a little time to gain enough confidence in the rest of us to talk about his own circumstances. The talk had been about family, household chores, support networks, how there was nothing good on the telly any more, the loneliness of evenings, times of wistfulness and tears, and much more.

Towards the end of our time together I asked if there was anything we hadn't touched on that it would be helpful to explore. There was a silence for a bit, then Tommy spoke. 'My daughter's nippin' my head about the wife's clothes.' He went on to explain that he had not as yet been able to clear out his wife's clothes, to take them to a local charity shop, or the like. He couldn't face dealing with it because he wasn't ready yet. It was too final an issue to face, too permanent. And he didn't need the space anyway. So he left them where they were. His daughter, on the other hand, saw this as her dad 'being stuck', not facing up to reality, not moving on. She needed a sign, a public sign, that things were progressing for her dad. But, as far as the clothes were concerned, it just wasn't coming from that direction. So she was nagging him, 'nipping his head', and he didn't like it at all.

'What am I supposed to do?' he asked. 'I don't need the space. It's too much to get ma head round.' He paused, and leaned forward as if to draw us into his confidence. 'If fact, to tell you the truth, sometimes I open the wardrobe door an' hae a look at the clothes, just to remind me o' the wife, ken?' I nodded, and so did the other two men. But before I had the chance to offer reassurance with something like, 'That's just fine, Tommy, it's quite normal,' he leaned even further forward, and, with a voice barely above a whisper, he said, 'Actually – an' even ma daughter disnae ken this – sometimes I take some of the clothes out o' the wardrobe an' I smell them, for I ken that's how the wife used tae smell.' He was red in the face, and sat back in his seat as if some great burden had fallen from his shoulders. And, again, before I had a chance to offer anything more, George said, 'Well, maybe it'll surprise you to hear that that's just what I do too.' And Jim, who had sat quietly through all of this, uttered the immortal and ultimately healing words, 'Jesus Christ, an' so do I!' They all laughed, and nodded sagely, and the job was done. And I remember the three men continuing their conversation in the hospice car-park long after the groups were finished for that evening. Obviously there was more useful sharing and comparing of notes going on!

These three men, in this facet of their bereavement journey, had been isolated in their reactions to loss till that moment, feeling strange and perhaps somewhat ashamed in doing something that felt right and spontaneous but could, they thought, be viewed as a little bizarre. These three men, with the world – in the shape of a concerned daughter 'nipping ma head' – so keen that they exhibit signs that they were moving on, had been able to be honest about their stories. Prompted by the trust that had been created, drawn out by the risky choice one of them had made to be out-front about his circumstances, they had found a normalising and, indeed, a healing of their journey. All three were much relieved. I could see that. And, I suspect, Tommy went right home to tell his daughter to stop nipping his head about his wife's clothes because two other guys were handling things in exactly the same way.

At the conclusion of that group, I told the three men the story of Len, a young man whom we had worked with some years before, who'd lost his wife at a relatively young age. One evening, coming up to the anniversary of his wife's death, I asked Len and the folk in his group if anything had happened in the past month they wanted to share or clarify. There was talk of a holiday being booked, a birthday that had been hard, a visit to a relative, and the like. And when it was Len's turn, he said, 'I've changed the name-plate on the front door.' He was about to move on to something else, when I stopped him. 'Wait a minute,' I said, 'that seems quite significant, a big step forward.' 'No,' he replied, 'no big deal. I just changed the name plate. I realised that it said "Mr and Mrs" and that that wasn't the case any more. So I went down to the hardware shop and got a new one that just said "Mr".' 'Wow,' I responded, 'that does seem like a big thing to do.' 'No,' Len insisted, 'I just changed the name-plate because I realised it was wrong.'

Len had passed that name-plate hundreds of times since his wife had died. There it was, 'Mr and Mrs', wrong from the day his wife had passed away. But he didn't need to change it. It wasn't the time. There was no need. Or perhaps it hadn't even been noticed, never absorbed by his conscious mind. Until one day, months after the death, he realised it was wrong, sorted it out, and moved on. 'No big deal' was right enough, because an issue had been dealt with in the right way at the right time, with no external or personal pressure or expectations, no conforming to whatever norms existed, no fitting a preconceived or 'nipping ma head' pattern. It's a lesson for all who are bereaved, is it not?

The other value of ongoing bereavement support is simply the continuous nature of it. I can recall a number of occasions in my ministry over the years – too many, and some of them too painful even yet to talk about – when the pressure of immediate pastoral demands, work issues, family matters, crises to contend with, other people to care for, other deaths to cope with, served to push into the background the need, indeed the necessity, for my ongoing contact with those who were bereaved. If society gives us only six weeks to grieve, how much more important it is, therefore, for people – someone, anyone – to make contact with the bereaved long after everyone else has forgotten. 'Oh, it will make them upset. I don't want to open up old wounds.' Rubbish! People are upset anyway. They live with their upset every day. And they have seen people walk away. They have heard people make promises that remain unfulfilled – including some from me. And they are all the more isolated in their loss.

Why do we not make contact? Because the immediate is more demanding and, perhaps, more stimulating to our caring role, while the grind of caring over time is not nearly as attractive; and because, far from creating pain for those we visit, we are avoiding our own pain by staying away. So – and I have to keep reminding myself of this ('Physician, heal thyself' indeed!) – go to visit, make a phone call, write that card, remember the anniversary – and the second one and the third one – share a word, shake the hand, give your hug of comfort. Whatever you do, don't avoid the moment. People know what they're living with. You'll not make it worse by entering their world. But you might unknowingly make it a lot worse, you might unfeelingly compound the problem, by choosing to stay away.

Supporting people month after month in our bereavement support groups not only reassures them that they and their journey of loss still matter to others long after most folk no longer mention it, but also gives us the opportunity to affirm how far these individuals have come on their journey. Take Don, for example. He had been married for 59 years. He and his wife, Aggie, had been inseparable. Now he was left alone, bereft of his life-companion, his carer, his soulmate, his cook, his confidante, and much, much more besides. (Don't let anyone tell you that bereavement is a single loss when it carries with it many losses which have all to be endured at once.) When Don first attended our groups on a Thursday afternoon, he couldn't speak a word. Every time he was addressed, drawn into the conversation, even looked at, he would weep copiously. People were very sensitive to him and gave him a lot of support. We didn't think he would come back because it had obviously been too difficult for him. But he did. The next time he came he had with him a poly-bag, and in it he had pictures of Aggie – when he first met her, on their wedding day, and many more, up to some holiday snaps taken not long before she took ill. Again, those in the group were sympathetic and tolerant, and this time Don could talk about his wife, mention her name through his tears, and then say nothing for a while more.

In time, Don came to the end of his participation in our support system, and, just after the anniversary of Aggie's death, he attended his final group. He confessed to feeling that he was still struggling, and that he didn't feel things had progressed all that much. One of the women in the group had been around when Don had first come. 'Aye,' she said wisely, 'we all struggle, if we're honest, and we don't get on as quickly as we would like. But if you remember what you were like when you first started to come here, when you couldn't speak for crying, and look at you now, then you've come an awful long way, right enough.' Don smiled. 'Aye, I think you're right.' And another job had been done.

I remember Lorna coming to the groups for the first time after her partner had died. She couldn't lift her eyes off the floor. She couldn't look any one of us in the eye. Over the months, with commitment from her and with a lot of support and understanding from other people, she began to respond and to engage with the issues of her loss. I recall one evening struggling to draw her into our conversations. She'd said she'd had a bad week, but didn't say why. She didn't contribute much, choosing to listen in silence. I was worried about her and kept a watchful eye on her as I and the others talked. However, I stopped worrying half way through the discussion when one of the group was reflecting on an issue she'd been dealing with recently and how it had been resolved. I can't now remember what it was or what was said. But I do remember Lorna lifting her head, looking the other woman in the eye, nodding gently, and breaking into the hint of a smile. Someone had understood. She recognised that someone had insights into her problem. Healing words now forgotten in the mists of time. But a healing moment that had been important to Lorna.

The months went by, and Lorna was in my group as the anniversary of her bereavement approached. She told me she still wasn't coping well, but then went on to recount a tale of something silly that had happened at work that week. Everyone laughed – another healing moment – and I remember reminding Lorna later that evening of how things had been back in those early months of her loss. We compared the now with the then, and she confessed she couldn't even remember what she had done or said that first night, and no mention was made of the healing moment she'd experienced some months later. But she did know what we all knew, that healing had been happening all the time, and, despite her continued struggles, things were better than they had been at the start.

Then there was Edith, who told us one evening that she had just realised, nine months after her mother's death, that 'The family have stopped talking about mum. It's as if she never existed,' and that this was the only place where she felt that her mum could still be remembered. And I recall the look of delight on her face as she realised that the people in the group were interested in hearing about her mother. And in the using of her name, in the sharing of her personality, in the telling of her stories, Edith's mother was real again, and Edith herself was animated and alive.

So people need to find those healing words and healing moments, in the recognition that their patterns of grief are acceptable, that they can be compared positively with those of other people, that they are taken seriously, that they are not forgotten, that they still matter. Time does indeed heal. Or should we better say that people find healing in their loss over time? And how long does it take? Only time will tell.

There are times, too, when those moments of healing take people by surprise, and, when handled with intuition and not following some theory or set pattern, they are real stepping stones on the journey of bereavement. Harry, a widower in his later sixties, told me once of what had been a very 'wobbly' moment at home a few days before. He had lost his wife about nine months previously, and while he felt he was progressing pretty well, he struggled with emotion from time to time. The previous Wednesday afternoon, his eight-year-old grandson Bobby had come round after school like he often did, as the old man and wee boy enjoyed each other's company. Sometimes they watched TV together, often Bobby would help his granddad in the garden, and occasionally he would ask questions about his gran. 'Is granny in heaven?' he had asked one day. To which Harry told me he had replied – with tears in his eyes – 'Aye, she is right enough, son, for heaven'll no' be much o' a place if your granny's no' there.'

On this particular wet Wednesday, Bobby had asked his granddad if he could watch a video. So, while Harry got some fizzy and biscuits organised in the kitchen, Bobby got a video-tape sorted out. Then, Harry told me, he couldn't believe what he was hearing. It was his wife's voice. Clear as a bell, laughing, shouting, chatting, from the next room. For a moment – a long-wished-for moment – she was alive, ready to welcome him with wee Bobby when he went through with the tray. And, just as quickly, the moment was gone as reality hit home. Trembling slightly, he put his head round the door of the lounge, and there he found his grandson sitting cross-legged in front of the TV, watching a holiday video of the whole family in Majorca. And there, in the fullness of life, was Harry's beloved Jean.

He was transfixed. He was deeply moved. After a while Bobby turned around, aware of his granddad behind him, and Harry, thinking the young lad would be distressed by the images and wanting to protect him from the sorrow and heal a difficult moment, said to him, 'Did you put the wrong tape in by mistake, son?' 'No, granddad,' the wee boy replied, 'I needed to see granny again and remember what she was really like. I hope you don't mind.' So Harry joined Bobby on the floor, and granddad and grandson spent a few more moments watching and talking about a lovely granny and wife, and laughing and crying as they did so. And soon, when the video was over, it was fizzy and biscuits time with talk of school and football and gardens, and life moved on.

I asked Harry what he made of all of that. 'What do I make of it?' he asked. 'It was wonderful, a real special moment.' 'Destructive?' I asked. 'Could have been,' he responded. 'But then, Bobby made it so natural, so easy. You see, he was ahead o' me. Ah've got pictures in ma head a' the time, ma ain tapes ah can run and rerun. He husnae got a' that. So he needed a reminder. And ah was chuffed tae bits that he'd want tae dae it on purpose, tae choose to watch ma Jean. It was just lovely, me and the wee laddie, and Jean there wi' us baith, in the fullness o' life.' A child ahead of an adult, right enough, and, with intuition, getting it right. An adult learning from a child, and, by intuition, sharing a healing moment. And for both of them, a granny and a wife was remembered, brought to mind, talked about and held close.

Healing moments aren't always predictable, like the one Margo contrived to create, but one which, I must confess, initially filled me with horror. Margo was Ukrainian. Actually her name wasn't Margo, but she had become so fed up over the years with people spelling and pronouncing her Ukrainian name in bizarre ways she eventually gave in and started using a shortened, anglicised form. And Margo was an extraordinary woman. She was loud, larger-than-life, and wore, as I recall, the most extraordinary make-up. Her husband had died in the hospice, and we had got to know Margo and her big personality during the short time he was with us. And, of course, Margo came to our bereavement support groups. Actually, she only came a couple of times. Her need was simply to come back to the place her husband Boris had died, to touch base with the staff who had cared for him, and to say thank-you – in a loud and here's-a-huge-box-of-chocolates kind of way, absolutely appropriate to her approach to things and her circumstances.

I happened to have Margo in my group the final time she was with us. In the group were a mother and daughter and two other widows, one of whom was with us for the first time. It had been a good group, with lots of useful sharing in which Margo had played a helpful part. As we were breaking up, Margo announced, 'Before go, I show pictures of Boris. I have pictures of Boris here in hand-bag. You wait now, I show pictures.' Nice, I thought. Like Don, a chance for others to see a loved one. Like Edith, a chance for some-one to talk about a loved one. Like Bobby and Harry, a chance to remember what someone was really like. So we waited patiently while Margo unearthed the packet of photographs from the deep recesses of her cavernous handbag. Eventually, all was ready. 'So, here pictures. Here pictures of Boris,' she announced. 'Here picture of Boris coffin at graveside.' *'No!'* I screamed inside. *'This cannot be happening. This is not what you do, Margo. No. No! Please, no more!'* 'And here picture of Boris coffin being lowered into grave,' she continued. *'O my God, we're going to have a picture of an open coffin. I know we are. This will destroy everything. These other people will be reduced to tears.'* 'All pictures taken by friend, Ukrainian friend, to send back to Kiev to family not able to get to funeral. Here picture of priest saying prayers for Boris. Here flowers from family. Here all people who came to cemetery for Boris. And here people getting into big limousines to go back to house for tea.'

Eventually the picture show was over and I was released from my torment. And I realised, to my amazement, that the others in the group were fully involved with Margo and the photographs. Comments such as, 'O, lovely day you got, Margo. What cemetery was that?' 'Young priest, don't you think. Good looking young man. Ukrainian, is he? Good service?' 'Lovely flowers' and 'What family is there over in Kiev, Margo? I'm sure they'll appreciate the photos. What a lovely thing to do' served to reassure me that, far from Margo's boldness with the pictures destroying anything, what she had done was create another amazing, healing moment, even though it was beyond my experience and comprehension. And why? Because no one judged. No one said no. Everyone – including me, eventually – saw the point. And Margo, and the rest of us, had been helped on our way, by healing words and a healing moment that even I didn't expect.

Several years after my mother's death, when I had begun to look again at my bereavement journey and how inadequately I had handled it, I learned some lessons which have never left me. One of these was that there are healing moments in life which can become increasingly important in bereavement. Things said, reconciliations worked at, contacts re-established, love shared, when people are well enough to hear and take on board what is being said and done, can 'finish the business' and, in time, give a firmer foundation to the processes of bereavement.

My father and I were never particularly demonstrative with each other. There was deep love and respect. There was pride and admiration from both sides. But there was the firm handshake when we met, with no additional expressions in word and action of our affection for each other. That's the way it was. But, as I thought about things at a deeper level, I came to understand that there was something unfinished between me and my dad. There were things I needed to say before it was too late. I couldn't say them to his face – that would have been too hard for us both. So I decided to write my dad a letter. It was short and to the point, but it said all I needed to say. I told him how good a dad he'd been, how I valued his support, and how I was pleased he was my father and the grandfather of my children. I went as far as I felt able to. And the letter was posted and I waited for a response. I got none.

I spoke with my dad on the phone every Sunday evening. The first Sunday after I'd sent the letter, I waited for him to say he'd got it, but he never did. The next Sunday, no mention either. Well, I thought, it's got lost in the post, or he's felt I've gone too far, or it's been OK but he can't bring himself to say so. So I stopped expecting him to mention it. What was done was done. That was, until some months later ...

My dad had come to spend a week's holiday with us. He was in good form. One day, I passed him on the stairs, as he was coming down from his bedroom and I was going upstairs. 'OK, son?' he asked. 'Not bad,' I replied, and we both continued on our way. Then, he stopped, half turned round, and said over his shoulder, 'Oh, by the way, thanks for your letter,' and carried on down the stairs. That was enough. The acknowledgement was all I required. The letter was never mentioned again. There was no need.

When my father died, I found the letter in his wallet in the inside pocket of his jacket. It had never left his possession since he'd got it. A healing moment in life became a healing moment in another bereavement journey. 'We cannot measure how you heal or answer every sufferer's prayer'[41], but we can certainly know that healing when it happens to us.

Notes

40   Henry James (1843–1916), from *The Ambassadors*, book 5, chapter 2.

41   John L Bell and Graham Maule, 'We cannot measure how you heal', from *Love From Below*, published by Wild Goose Publications, ISBN 094798870X.

Healing tears

I cried today – a gentle cry,
a falling tear,
just brushed away so no one noticed.
No sobbing grief,
no heartfelt cry of pain,
no sorrow's anguish bursting forth.
I cried today – a gentle cry,
and shed a loving tear.

I cried today – a gentle sign
of being at one with sorrow,
deeply felt;
a pain with ease expressed,
an anguished brokenness so ill concealed.
I cried today – a gentle sign,
because I understood the feelings there
of others' grief.

You cried today – a gentle cry,
a falling tear of present love I hardly noticed.
I'd looked for signs that you were there,
and almost missed your tender touch,
your falling tear.
You cried today – a gentle cry,
and showed, with tender tears,
a love that understood.

You cried today – a gentle sign
of incarnation here,
of being at one with sorrow deeply felt;
a pain with ease expressed,
an anguished brokenness so ill concealed.

You cried today - a gentle sign,
because you understand the feelings here
of grief like ours.

We cried today – a gentle cry
as mingled tears with misty sighs in silence fell.
No hopeless grief,
no unheard cry of pain,
no sorrow's anguish threatening life and love.
We cried today – our gentle cry
had healed that moment when
our love was shared and shown in tears.

You came

I saw you look
with wonder in your eyes,
questioning the 'why' of me,
and whether you should come,
and meet me
here and now.

I saw you turn
to make the opening move,
still with uncertain 'will' or 'won't'
and tensions in your heart,
to see beyond the 'why'
and come.

I saw you come,
with tiny, tip-toe steps.
Too quick for you, too slow for me,
the gap was closed,
for you,
and now for me.

I saw your smile,
the warmth and welcome in your face,
no words,
just love no words could show,
embracing me,
the me you know.

I saw your hand,
lie gently close to mine,
permissively,
so I could reach,
and touch your fingers there,
and take your hand in mine.

I saw your fear
fade quickly from your searching eyes,
for now you know,
the risk
was worth the taking
in the sharing here.

I felt you heal
my lonely, broken, dis-eased soul,
with what you are,
and what you now must know,
that in your coming here
I have been loved again.

I saw you go,
and let you go to share your love once more,
with someone else
who needs to know
your love
can heal them too.

I promised

I promised, said I.
I know, said God.
I failed, said I.
I know, said God.
I'll try, said I.
I know, said God.
I know, said I.
I promise, said God.

Ten

Anger again

'He is trampling out the vintage where the grapes of wrath are stored'
Julia Ward Howe: 'Mine eyes have seen the glory ...'

'You purchase pain with all that joy can give,
And die of nothing but a rage to live'
Alexander Pope: 'To a lady'

On most of the occasions when I'm asked to give talks or lead seminars and workshops on issues of grief and loss, in whatever setting and with whatever group of people, we end up talking about anger. In some form, with some story, with some remembrance of vehemence, we end up talking about the way anger, in its various expressions, is integral to the processes of grief and loss. Out of people's own experiences, and as they recall and struggle with the experiences of others, they know that anger and bereavement go together. It may not manifest itself in violent expressions like my screaming at Talbot's death. But anger is there, doing its subtle, destructive best to threaten our growth and ability or desire to move on. There are times, as Alexander Pope suggests, when we have 'but a rage to live'42, when we know what anger means, and when we are all too familiar with it as a dominant human emotion.

Anger is part of the journey of loss. I have already spoken of Glenda's anger at Clive's death and, indeed, her anger at her husband for leaving her with unfulfilled hopes and dreams. My poem 'Sainsbury's', at the end of the earlier chapter exploring aspects of being out of control in one's loss, comes from a specific incident recounted to me by a bereaved relative. It illustrates the ferocious anger welling to the surface when a bereaved person was struggling to do shopping shortly after a death, when other people were enjoying themselves at the same time. Indeed, it is an experience I have had myself, as I sought to get back to some kind of normality after my own bereavements.

Not surprisingly, there is also the anger that is directed at God, a God who is perceived to do something, or not to do something, or to allow something to happen, that leaves people with the pain of loss. This is an anger that is very real and expressed by people of a deep religious faith and none. If we perceive that we are having to cope with a God who exhibits 'the grapes of wrath'[43], then you can be sure that God will get the full force of our anger in return. And there are times when, if people can't get at God, they get at God's representative! I know this is not confined to hospice or hospital chaplaincies but is common in the interaction of all pastors and religious leaders with those who are struggling to understand suffering, pain, death and loss. You don't like the message so you shoot the messenger. How many times have I experienced an anger at God which was being directed at me with all its attendant vehemence? Never mind the 'grapes of wrath' of God. What about the grapes of wrath of his angry people? A common experience? Oh yes, but not a nice one, I can tell you!

Yet, in a paradoxical way, I like it when people are angry with God. For at least that means they are being real, and not seeing their faith as a kind of divine bubble-wrap which protects them from the bashing and rough handling of the delivery processes of life. And even when it means I'm in the firing line, it's got to be better than hearing 'Well, it's just God's will,' when I believe it isn't.

These two offerings from *Friends and Enemies: A book of short prayers and how to write your own*[44], and a third from John O'Donohue's book, *Eternal Echoes: Exploring our hunger to belong*[45], serve to illustrate the point. Firstly, this honest offering, 'A regrettable prayer', from Ian Cowie:

Good God,
what a mess!
Father,
come and collect your lost child.
Jesus,
come and deal with your disciple who gets things wrong.
Holy Spirit,
come and refill this body, your temple.
Over to you, God,
I'm in your hands now.
What will you make of me?
Back to square one at this time of my life?
O Christ!

And then, this heartfelt prayer, 'Why?', from the pupils of Hackwood Park School, a school for children with moderate learning difficulties near Hexham in Northumberland:

Why do you let people die if you love us?
Why do you let people hurt and cry inside?
Why do you let people get cuts and bruises?
Why do you let people have nasty accidents?

And finally, this reflection on suffering by John O'Donohue:

Suffering is frightening. It unhouses and dislocates you. Suffering is the
arrival of darkness from an angle you never expected. There are different
kinds of darkness. There is the night where the darkness is evenly brushed.
The sky is studded with the crystal light of stars and the moon casts mint
light over the fields. Though you are in the darkness, your ways are guided
by a gentle light. This is not the darkness of deep suffering. When real
suffering comes, the light goes out completely. There is nothing but a forsaken
darkness, frightening in its density and anonymity ... The dark squall of

suffering dismantles belonging and darkens the mind. It rips the fragile net of meaning to shreds. Like a dark tide it comes in a torrent over every shoreline of your inner world. Nothing can hold it back. When you endure such a night, you never forget it. When you stand in the place of pain, you are no-one. There is a poignant line from Virgil's Aeneid describing one of the heroes found dead in anonymous circumstances: 'corpe sine nomine' i.e. a body without a name. Belonging is shredded ... You are utterly unhoused. Now you know where Nowhere is. No one can reach you. Suffering seems to be a force of primal regression. It almost wipes your signature as an individual and reduces you to faceless clay. Suffering is raw, relentless otherness coming alive around you and inside you.

Is it any wonder, therefore, that such suffering calls forth a response of anger, from the prayer of a struggling soul, through the honesty of children, to the word-picture of being 'unhoused' by the dislocation and devastation such suffering brings? And is it any wonder that in the face of such suffering, from all humanity and for all time, God gets the brunt of our rage?

So anger, in its many forms and manifestations, is real and right. Not just the out-of-control, screaming and raging anger, the punching-the-wall and banging-your-head-on-the-pillow anger, but the subtle, irritable, seething-inside anger we all know so well. There's the anger that is expressed at medical staff for breaking bad news about a terminal illness or for being the one who has had to tell a family that their loved one has now died. Of course there are times when professionals don't do things right or when they handle situations badly. And where criticism and challenge are appropriate, then it is to be hoped that with anger reasonably well under control healthcare professionals should be questioned and situations of uncertainty clarified. But often anger is simply what ministers get when people can't get at God; it's the 'I-don't-like-the-message-so-I'll-shoot-the-messenger' anger. We all get that, and it has to be seen and worked with for what it is – a lashing out, a vehement reaction to bad news or death, directed at whoever happens to be in the way.

When we work with bereaved people at the start of their journey of loss, such anger has to be taken seriously and not pushed away. If a bereaved relative needs to talk through the final days and hours with a doctor or nurse who cared for their loved one, and even to go over the patient's notes in order to get their head round what has happened, then that is what needs to be done. And mostly that's enough, for a relative is simply trying to come to terms with the situation, trying to get things in order in their mind, and doing so dissipates the anger against individuals and allows the bereaved person to see it for what it really is, an expression of anger at death itself. When they identify the root of the anger, they can work with it and can be helped to move on. But when the anger is argued with, or dismissed, or pushed away, then it can become an even more destructive force and will begin to slow down the grief process, deflecting people from dealing with what it is really all about.

The more common kind of anger is that which is illustrated in Glenda's story, the anger at being left alone and having to adapt to a new beginning. I have lost count of the number of times when, in working with bereaved partners, someone will say how hard it is to begin to relate again to a society and a social life that is largely 'couple-based'. There is an irrational anger which rises within a grieving partner at the very fact of another couple being together and enjoying themselves. It is the cry of pain, the rising anger, the natural selfishness of grief, which comes from the question 'Why me?', and indeed, if we are honest, 'Why not someone else?' Of course that couple holding hands in the street, or pushing a trolley round Sainsbury's, or sitting in front of you at the theatre are not purposely flaunting their 'coupleness' to hurt you in your loss. But that's how it feels, doesn't it? Anger is an irrational, but natural, response.

There is the anger too – and the confusion that is at the root of it

– of a partner having to learn new roles in their loss, when they are emotionally at a low ebb anyway, and without the energy or commitment to work at taking on new tasks. Simon was left widowed at the age of 32. He had two wonderful daughters, aged eight and ten, and they had all coped remarkably well with the loss of Jane, a devoted wife and mother. After a spell off work on compassionate grounds, Simon went back to his office. Childcare had been organised, grandparents and neighbours had rallied round, and everything was as good as it could be in trying circumstances. Simon was committed to his new role and his new tasks, organising meals, juggling where the girls should be and when, keeping the household and its affairs in order, as well as holding down a responsible job and dealing with the practical and emotional aftermath of Jane's death.

Public holidays were spent having fun with the children. School holidays were a flurry of arrangements, and worries about childcare, and time with grandparents, and rushing from place to place. Work was stressful and the company expected Simon, now months after his bereavement, to function as normal, to put in extra hours, to take on additional responsibilities, to be on top of everything all of the time. It was as if they had forgotten about his loss and his present circumstances, or, if they hadn't, they didn't want to know any more. They just wanted him to be an up-to-the-mark employee, and if he couldn't hack it, that was his problem and not theirs. And Simon was becoming exhausted.

I knew all this because he asked me to come to see him one day. He'd been signed off work for a few days with 'flu – a legitimate reason not to be at the office for which he was most thankful – and he had time to think a bit about things. He needed someone to listen to his woes. 'No one else seems to be bothered asking any more,' he told me. He needed help to make sense of what was happening to him. And as his story tumbled out, and as the past few months' anxieties were heaped in an ever-growing pile in front of him, he began to get more and more angry. Until, like a rumbling volcano, he burst forth in a veritable explosion of feelings. 'I hate it, I hate being like this,' he cried. 'I hate the girls. I hate the time they take and the importance they have to have. I hate having no time, no space, no freedom. I hate being left like this.' I had nothing to say. He was right, of course, and though it wasn't anyone's fault that this was the way things were to be, the anger had to be expressed somehow. Of course he didn't hate his children, for he was too good a father for that. But he hated what they represented, that he now had sole responsibility for their welfare, and it was wearing him down. I don't now recall what I said or what we went on to talk about. Maybe allowing him to be in touch with his anger was enough. But I do remember vividly what was in front of me that day, a rightly angry man, who at least had the sense and the awareness to express what he was feeling and to share with someone what he was going through.

That, in a very real sense, is the key to dealing with this kind of anger. If it is not to be pushed away but acknowledged as a right response, then one has to allow it expression, to be put somewhere. People need to have their anger acknowledged as real, and see that acknowledgement as the beginning, hopefully, of a healing process. I didn't much like what I was hearing from Simon on that day. I didn't really want to be there and to be faced with his vehemence. The fallout from a volcano can be damaging. But I hope that, for Simon, his sharing of his anger was what it needed and seemed to be, a catharsis that created a stepping stone to a new beginning.

There is another kind of anger that we meet in bereavement work. Let Betty tell you her story. Betty was a widow in her early fifties. I knew her and her family when I was a young minister. She and Tommy, her husband, had eight children, the eldest just turned thirty, and the youngest still in primary school. Several of the children were still at home, surviving in a crazy but ultimately supportive household. Actually, there was another wee one tagged on to the bottom end of the family, for Betty and Tommy were also bringing up a baby who was the product of a night – or even several nights – of passion between her 17-year-old daughter and the lad next door.

Tommy died of a heart attack at the age of 57. This harum-scarum family coped remarkably well as families often do, just getting on with things and realising that there was no choice but to move forward. It wasn't that there was no grief – there was bucket-loads of that around – or that life was cheap: Tommy had been a good man and was sorely missed. It was just that there was a family to care for, and wee ones to feed and organise, and recalcitrant teenagers to cope with, and the rest. Most of that responsibility fell on Betty's broad shoulders. Not that she was unsupported by her older girls, but, as she said herself, 'They've got their own families and I can't go runnin' to them all the time. I just have to knuckle down and get on with it. Life owes me no favours.'

So Betty did get on with it, and did a remarkably good job. Until, that is, nine months or so had passed. I happened to bump into her at the shops one afternoon, and she looked terrible. She had always looked tired – family life had always been busy even before Tommy died – but now she looked worn out. I suggested I come to see her, and in a rare quiet half-hour, between picking up kids from school and sorting out the house, she told me what was happening. 'I feel I'm going backwards,' she said. 'I was doin' so well. I felt I'd cracked it. But the last couple of months have been really hard. I just can't get out of the bit. It's gettin' worse rather than better. An' I was doin' fine, as well. I shouldn't be like this. I have to keep goin' for the kids. If I crack up, what'll happen to them? I'm so angry with myself. I should be doin' better than this.'

For Betty, her busyness, her necessary busyness, had been a bless-ing and a curse, the salvation and the problem at one and the same time. For her need to 'keep goin' for the kids' had given her purpose, drive, commitment, call it what you will. It did, indeed, keep her going and was a real purpose to live for. But it was also the problem, for it was wearing her out, and it wasn't allowing her to grieve for her loss. So she had been carried forward on a wave of busyness, and that had been OK. But now, perhaps with tiredness as the root cause, the emotional reality was beginning to dawn. Tommy was gone for good; the reality was that this was permanent; this was the way it was always going to be from now on. And that reality had crept up on her, and was now greatly threatening her equilibrium.

There was, in fact, nothing wrong with Betty, and her journey of loss hadn't gone off course. She was experiencing what many people tell us about, that when the permanent nature of the loss hits home, sometimes months after the death, then it leaves you feeling worse, and it's as if you have started to go backwards. Add into that mix what Betty hadn't been able take on board, or indeed hadn't had space to realise was important – that she'd just come through what would have been her and Tommy's 35th wedding anniversary, and, as she thought back on it, that this week was the anniversary of the first time Tommy had been signed off work with pains in his chest. It was no wonder she was having a bad time.

Often people in loss get angry with themselves because they feel they are going backwards when they were doing so well, and that they should be able to do something about it. Indeed, it's because they have perceived themselves to be doing well that they see it as their fault that they can't continue to do so; they feel that this 'slipping back' is reversible, that it's something they can and should rectify, and if they can't, they're to blame. Not so. What is happening is not of their making. Betty did not cause, nor could she change, her period of struggle. For her it was necessary and normal. It was another stage in coming to terms with the reality of her loss. She was angry with herself for failing. But she needn't have been, for she had not failed – and indeed had done, and continued to do, remarkably well.

Anger in the journey of grief, as I have already said, takes many forms which, in their expression of the devastation of loss, have to be understood and worked with. Let me conclude, therefore, with another example of anger. This anger, had it not been understood and seen for what it was, could have become destructive to relationships and the healing of the grief journey. Thankfully, it didn't.

Cindy was a delightful young woman. She and her husband Pat had come over to Edinburgh from Dublin with Pat's job, his company inviting him to do some 'troubleshooting' in their Scottish office, necessitating a short-term relocation just outside Edinburgh with Rachel, their three-year-old daughter. Six months had stretched into a year, one year into two, and a temporary position became a permanent posting. They had just bought a house in a new development, and Rachel was settled in the first year of primary schooling. Things were looking good. Then Pat took ill, seriously ill, with an aggressive and incurable cancer. He died two weeks after Rachel's sixth birthday.

It does not need me to unfold how hellish all of this was for Cindy and both her and Pat's families. You can, I suspect, feel the devastation out of your own experience and your understanding of the human condition. Simply put, it was just unspeakably terrible. Pat's funeral took place back in Ireland, largely organised and directed by his family. My involvement with Cindy was to be around to allow her to talk, to make sure her wishes and feelings were taken into consideration in all the funeral arrangements, and to be available to her when she came back to Edinburgh to try to begin to makes sense for her and Rachel of a life without Pat.

She phoned me a few days after she got back from Dublin, and we met up to talk about things. She unfolded the whole story about the funeral, what had gone well and what hadn't, what she had felt was helpful and what wasn't, whose words were supportive and whose weren't, and much more. She just needed to offload all of her jumbled thoughts and emotions and know that someone would listen. All through her story, her mother-in-law Teresa figured very highly. She and Cindy had never really got on. They had learned to be polite and dignified with each other over the years, but there were still underlying resentments and tensions, some of which had resurfaced during Pat's illness. It seemed that Teresa hadn't approved of Pat's choice of wife in the first place. She was English, not Irish, and, Cindy told me, that made her feel that she 'wasn't one of them'. They had been married in a Registry Office and not in a Catholic church as Pat's family expected. They had moved to Scotland, away from family roots, and Cindy had been made to feel that she was responsible for taking a son away from his mother.

As families do, they had learned to live with all of that, creating as peaceful a co-existence as possible and working round the tensions. And that is fine, until a crisis arises or a trauma rocks a family's equilibrium – just what had happened in Pat's illness and dying. Teresa was a constant visitor at Pat's bedside. There was a clear sense of 'competition' as a mother losing her only son and a wife losing her young husband 'vied' for central position. Of course they were still polite – social conventions determined that – but the tensions had been palpable.

So it was that in unfolding the story of the events of Pat's funeral, Teresa's name came up again and again. And the more she was mentioned, the angrier Cindy became. There was anger at things said, attitudes adopted, things done and not done, pressure exerted both overtly and subtly, and at promises made about what the future might or might not hold. And the more Teresa became the focus of this anger, the more demonised she became. I was aware that I was only getting one side of the story – though having met Teresa on a couple of occasions I had a certain sympathy for Cindy's feelings – but I was also aware of the fierce anger being expressed by this grieving and devastated young widow. So I listened, and allowed Cindy to tell her story with all the anger it contained. She needed to put that anger somewhere.

In the weeks that followed, Cindy and I returned to various aspects of her story, and, not surprisingly, to various aspects of her anger at Teresa. But, in time – after Cindy had convinced me that some of the anger was absolutely justified, and had therefore overcome her resistance to my helping her not to demonise her mother-in-law altogether – Cindy came to see her anger for what it was: a lashing-out, I-have-to-get-at-someone kind of anger, which was rooted in her anger at her loss. The anger at her loss was nebulous. It was like wrestling with mist. But Teresa was real and tangible. She was quantifiable and could be focused on. So she got the lot.

Cindy needed to see just what was happening to her, and to see her anger, wherever and however it was directed, as anger rooted in the death of her husband and the father of her child. I suspect, indeed I know, that if she had allowed herself to hang all the anger of her grief on the peg that had Teresa's name on it, she would have struggled to move through the grief process, and would have continued to 'externalise' her feelings, to blame someone else for what she was going through. Her grief journey, with anger as a component of it, had to include facing up to her own anger at her own loss, and not to focus it all on somewhere or someone else.

In time, Cindy was able to face Teresa with some of the issues which had caused her distress. She understood the tragedy of a mother losing her son and some aspects at least of the behaviour patterns which this created. But she could only do that when she was strong enough to handle it. That was when she had begun to deal with the roots of her anger and not dump it all on her mother-in-law. Cindy and Teresa never became bosom buddies. They weren't able to live happily ever after. They learned to accommodate each other in the wider family context and get back to workable social conventions. Teresa is still Rachel's grandmother and the mother of

Cindy's late husband; Cindy still has a mother-in-law whom she goes to visit and whom she loves for what she still offers to her little Rachel. So the anger in Cindy which had threatened to be destructive of a grief journey and of a set of family relationships has been understood and worked with, and people have moved on.

Alexander Pope's 'rage to live' is something we all know. Anger is part of our living and our grieving. So let's understand it and tackle it and name it and face it, so that, in some sense at least, we know we can come to be in control – yes, even of our anger.

Notes

42 Alexander Pope, from 'To a lady'.
43 From 'Mine eyes have seen the glory of the coming of the Lord' by Julia Ward Howe.
44 *Friends and Enemies*, ed. Ruth Burgess, Wild Goose Publications,
45 From *Eternal Echoes* by John O'Donohue, published by Bantam Press. Reprinted with permission of the Random House Group Ltd.

Creation speaks for me

I heard the wind,
the howl and scream,
the rage and shaking fist,
that shook the world.
I heard the wind,
and knew the angry gale
could speak for me.

I watched the waves,
the pounding surf,
and spreading, drenching spray
that drowned the rocks.
I watched the waves,
and knew the angry sea
could speak for me.

I felt the rain,
the biting shards
that harshly stung my face,
and drenched my dreams.
I felt the rain,
and knew the angry storm
could speak for me.

I heard the crash
of thunder claps
that made me shrink with fear,
this unseen power,
these thunder peals,
and knew the angry roar
could speak for me.

I saw the flash
of lightning fill the sky,
destructive force
of saw-toothed light.
When lightening struck,
I knew its violent surge
could speak for me.

Creation's voice,
in all its might
I knew could be my voice,
this angry roar,
can curse and rage
and all my anger show,
and speak for me.

My rage, my God

My rage!
My God,
but it's an awesome thing,
this ball of hate,
this cancerous lump
that fills me now
with all its hellishness.

My God!
This wild
ferocious beast that is
my anger now,
how can I hope
to ride the storm
this rage has brought to me?

My God,
will you
accept this offering
that curses you,
and hates your love,
and turns its back
on all that you will give?

My rage,
my God,
is all I have that's real;
I have no words,
no prayers to bring
that will make sense
of anything for now.

My God!
My rage
is me – the me that is
consumed by all
this hellishness.
So to my hell
reach out your hand for me.

And rage,
my God,
with me – and then give peace,
and hold for me
this anger now,
so I can know
this rage is understood.

Hiding my anger

Look –
I pull a curtain across my anger;
for it is mine,
too private for you to see.

Look –
I throw a cover over my rage;
for it is personal,
too intimate to be on view.

Look –
I cast a shroud around my fury;
for it is secret,
too disturbing to be on display.

And behind this curtain,
there is me and my anger –
real,
fierce,
truly mine,
in my privacy,
too obvious to hide.

And beneath this cover,
there is me and my rage –
wild,
uncontrolled,
part of me,
in intimacy,
too big to be ignored.

And within this shroud,
there is me and my fury –
vehement,

intense,
how I really am,
in disturbance,
too right to be ignored.

And you?
I ask only this of you –
that you wait for the curtain to be parted,
and be ready for the cover to be lifted,
and prepare yourself for the removal of the shroud.

For I need you then
to understand the anger,
and accept the rage,
and feel the fury.

For now you know
the private place,
the intimacy,
the reality of my very soul.

For now you know
that this is me.

So this I ask of you –
to wait
and watch
and understand,
till curtains close
and covers fall
and shrouds enclose again,
and remember
what you have glimpsed and known
of me,

what's real,
what's mine,
what's true,
and knowing anger lurks
behind my curtains drawn,
and love me still.

Eleven

Searching for the spirit

'Brutus: Then I shall see thee again?
Ghost: Ay, at Philippi.
Brutus: Why, I will see thee at Philippi, then.'
Shakespeare: 'Julius Caesar'

'Not far from Cirencester, was an apparition; being demanded whether a
good spirit or bad? Returned no answer.'
John Aubrey: 'Apparitions'

Julie contacted me just over a year after her father's death. I had
conducted her father's funeral, and while it was obviously a distressing event for Julie and the family, it wasn't what you would describe
as a difficult funeral or a particularly traumatic event. Jackie, her
father, had been 86 when he died. For some years he had lived two
doors up the street from Julie and her husband, having moved closer
to his daughter shortly after his wife had died. He had been largely
housebound in recent times, and while he could 'do for himself'
throughout the day, he relied on Julie to be his contact with the
outside world. She did his shopping, cleaned his house, organised his
laundry, put on his betting-line at the weekend. In short, she acted as
a devoted daughter, and without her there was no doubt that Jackie
would have needed a large package of care to keep him at home, or
indeed placement in long-term residential care.

Julie had worked for many years in a local school as a nursery
nurse. She loved her job and was good at it too, but holding down
full-time employment, running a family home, and being a dad's
carer and lifeline brought its times of tiredness and frustration. It was
hard to get a proper holiday, for example, as she had to arrange for

Jackie to go into respite care so she could get a break. He hated that – and told her so – and she just worried about him all the time she was away. However, most of the time she coped, and with good grace and commendable commitment she soldiered on.

In that sense, Julie was like countless other carers, fulfilling a responsibility, playing a role, 'doing her bit' for her father, and sometimes to her own detriment. But what was she to do? Stop caring? Not Julie, and not many, many others. So, each day she had a routine. Once she had finished in her own house, she would go down to the shops, get her dad's paper and pop in to see him before she went to work. She'd lay his breakfast table, organise his morning tablets, put on the fire in the living room to warm up the room for her dad coming down, and put her head round the bedroom door to see he was OK before she went off to work. Sometimes Jackie would be awake and ready to get up, other times he would be asleep and she would just leave him be. But she would know he was safe, and that everything was OK. Julie's husband popped in at lunchtimes to make the old man a sandwich, and after work Julie would be back again to make an evening meal and sort out other bits and pieces.

The day Jackie died had begun as normal. He hadn't been awake when Julie left, but everything looked fine. So, when she got a phone-call at work at lunchtime to say she should get home as soon as possible, she was cold with terror. Her worst fears were confirmed. Jackie had been found dead by his son-in-law. He was in his pyjamas on the bedroom floor. He'd probably been dead since just after Julie went away. He may even have been unwell before she left, but she'd never woken him up to ask. I remember Julie telling me this when we were arranging the funeral. As well as coping with the loss of her father, she was, as she put it, facing her own failure. She had let him down. Her father had died on his own, while she had been more concerned for other people's children than she was for her own flesh and blood.

I never heard much from Julie thereafter. One of my friends worked in the same nursery, so I would ask from time to time how she was getting on. The word was that she was fine, the odd wobbly day as you would expect, but on the whole she was doing fine. So I was surprised when she made contact with me again some months after the funeral, and I found myself in Julie's home once more talking over the events of Jackie's death. Despite her best efforts, the support and reassurance of her family, the attentiveness of her priest, and the understanding of her work colleagues, she could not disentangle herself from her sense of failure. It was affecting her health. She could function OK at work, and that, in many ways, had become her salvation. But the anniversary of her father's death had forced her to revisit his dying. And she could not shake off her overwhelming guilt.

Among other things, she told me she had been to a Spiritualist Church to see if her father would 'come through'. It hadn't resulted in contact with Jackie, but she was hopeful, very hopeful. It had happened to other people. You could see it on the telly. She needed it to happen for her. She talked about getting in touch with a medium to ask for a personal 'reading'. I asked her why. She cried when she told me that she needed to know from her father what he felt and when he had died. And she needed him to say that he was all right. She wanted to know that he was at peace. She could not rest within herself until she knew he was also at rest. 'Then I shall see thee again?'[46] She was searching for his spirit, so that his spirit could release her from her guilt.

I'll come back to Julie later, but her dilemma was and is not unusual. So often those that are left are tortured in their bereavement, or indeed torture themselves because of some unfinished business, some fractured relationship, or some sense of ultimate failure, so that they become weighed down with guilt as a result. None of us are perfect. Most of us live with unfinished business most of the time, and our relationships with each other are not tied up with red ribbon. They have many loose ends and frayed edges. And when death comes and what is unfinished is unfinished for ever, we try to learn to live with the ragged edges. In some sense at least we come to terms with the imperfect nature of our relationships and recognise that we were never going to get things right all of the time. But sometimes people in bereavement cannot find within themselves this capacity to learn to live with their unfinished business. So their guilt becomes their burden to carry and they come to feel that the only way they can move on is to be released from their guilt by the person who has gone. But now that the person has gone, how can we hear and accept words of forgiveness and be assured that our loved one is not tortured in death by our failure in life? So people who are bereaved often search for the spirit of the dead, seeking some word of comfort or consolation, some sense of reconciliation, so that, knowing the spirit of the dead person is at rest, they can live at peace themselves, find their own rest, and move on with their life.

While I was preparing this chapter, there was a series of programmes on TV about the work of mediums, and an exploration of many facets of what makes people sometimes so desperate to make contact with those who have 'passed over'. For some it is that deep-rooted curiosity, which is in all of us, to know if there is any proof that 'the other side' exists, that we have something to look forward to after death. Others are intrigued by a contact, or whether they might be contacted, singled out in effect, for some message from beyond the grave. But for many it is simply about searching for the spirit of the dead person because something is unfinished and needs to be resolved.

I recall in the TV series one man who had been contacted by his dead son, a young man killed in a road accident, and to whom he had never had the chance to say goodbye. His son told him he was fine and not to worry. And the father was overwhelmed with relief. That sounded fine to me, for I saw a grieving man being released from his torment and having the capacity to move on. But I also recall a woman whose son had committed suicide, and who went to meeting after spiritualist meeting in the hope that she could be in contact with him. And having been contacted once went back again and again, hoping, yearning for some more contact, without which, she said, she could not fully live. It did not take much for me to worry about this woman and her bereavement journey. Here was someone who had gone beyond the curiosity or even the unfinished business. Here was a woman who still needed her son to be here, who needed to believe he remained close, and who would hang on to any contact possible.

Yet you can see why people have these needs. And you can see the good and the bad sides of using this methodology to serve their bereavement journey. For myself, I have no problems with searching for the spirit in these ways. It does not challenge my religious beliefs, nor does it worry me in people's approach to bereavement. I have never personally felt the need to take this approach, but I have known it to be helpful to many people. So why deny its effectiveness when it is effective? Some years ago I worked with Billy, a lad who was one of the young leaders in a youth club. Billy's parents had married late, and he, an only child, had been born when his mother was in her forties and his father in his early fifties. So, now he was in his late teens, his father was well into retirement. One night when he was at the club with us he got a message that his father had died suddenly of a massive heart attack. The funeral a few days later was a big affair, the church full in support of a Kirk elder and his grieving family, and many of the mourners were there out of a genuine friendship with a popular local man.

Billy's mum didn't do too well in the early stages of her loss. And Billy was worried, even more so when he discovered his mum was planning to go to a Spiritualist meeting. 'Bloody mumbo-jumbo,' he ranted. 'All it'll do is mess up her head, as if she doesn't have enough going on at the moment!' Later that week, Billy took me aside at the youth club. 'Mum went to the meeting,' he whispered. 'How did she get on?' I enquired. 'Great!' he replied with raised eyebrows. 'She told me my dad made contact. He said he couldn't talk for long because of the earthquake in South America and because there were a lot of dead people and a lot of souls needing to be ferried over at the same time. But he said he was fine, and not to worry about the dog.' 'The dog?' 'Aye, Trixie, our spaniel. She'd been pining like hell since dad died. But he said not to worry because Trixie would be fine. And that was that. He was offski! Back to his apprentice-ferrying-of-souls stuff.' 'And your mother?' 'Absolutely fine! Never better! A changed woman ...' 'Do you think she'll go back?' 'She says she won't. No need. It's probably mumbo-jumbo, she says. But, whatever it is, she's a happier woman.' Over the months I got updates on the story. Billy told me that his mother had regained her equilibrium. Whatever had happened, she had 'turned a corner'. And Trixie had stopped pining too!

Believe it? Well, like me, you'll be wondering what all this is about. I don't know whether I believe that Billy's mum had been contacted by his dad. Billy didn't believe it at all. But what we both believed, because we both knew, was that one grieving woman had been helped to cope better with her grief, and one grieving dog was sorted too. And I for one am simply not prepared to argue with that kind of reality.

I want to suggest, however, that there are other ways to search for the spirit, to finish the business, to deal with issues of reconciliation, and the like. For those who remain sceptical about the world of mediums, for those who have tested this water and don't want to dive in, and for those who have utilised this framework in unhelpful ways as they seek to deny the reality of death, there are other methods. So, let me share with you part of my own story.

When my mother died following what should have been a

routine heart operation, the family were devastated. Death was not part of our expectations. What we believed we would have was a healthier, more active woman. What we were left with was the hell of bereavement. I have already unfolded some of my own bereavement journey following the death of my mother. But it is an evening before her death which is in my mind as I write this chapter. My mum had stayed with our family for a day so before her operation. She had come down from the north of Scotland to a big city hospital. We were her haven of refuge before her operation. So, on the appointed day, I took her into the hospital and saw her settled. I visited the following day, and on the night before her op went in to see her to make sure all was well. That evening I was rushed. I was late getting there and I had to dash away. My parting was cursory – I was a busy minister, my mother and I weren't particularly tactile with each other, and I didn't expect her to die. So, when I departed the ward, I left my mum sitting on the edge of her bed. She had her back to me as I glanced over my shoulder – no wave, no final words, no parting glance. And I was gone. I never saw my mother alive again.

Much later, as I revisited some issues in my life and what was driving me into patterns of attitude and behaviour, I took time with a supportive and sensitive counsellor to go back to that final interaction with my mother. I realised that it was disturbing me more than I knew, and that, having found it buried pretty deep in my psyche and festering away, it had to be exposed and sorted. I realised that I, too, was searching for the spirit. I had let my mother down in my unthinking and busy attitude. Like Julie, I had been more concerned for other people than for my own flesh and blood. I had failed my mother that night. And quite possibly I had screwed up completely and for ever. Being in contact with the spirit of my long-dead mother may have helped, and it may help even yet. But that approach wasn't for me either then or now, for I was helped to see that there was another way. That disastrous final evening with my mum could not be changed. What was would always be. But it could be revisited, looked at again, handled differently. Some reconciliation, some healing, could be found in the here and now, and not just through searching for contact with the spirit of a dead person.

The technique used with me is called 'visualisation'. What that means is being taken back into the situation which is of concern, visualising it in all its detail, describing it, painting a picture of it in words so that you can feel yourself back there again. For me, it was my mother's ward, and being back there again was painful, deeply emotional, and had to be handled very carefully. Then, out of my knowledge and understanding of my relationship with my mum – which only I knew, which only I could explain, which only I could make use of, and which only I could feel – I could visualise what might or could have happened differently.

I needn't go into all the details here, but I know how important it was. In my visualisation, as I paused at the door of the ward as I left my mother, I glanced back to see her, as indeed I had done at the time. But now my mother was turning round to watch me go. She said nothing, but she smiled, and in her smile she told me that she understood. So in this way I had been contacted, I had been living again with my mum, not in the spirit world, but in my ongoing relationship with her. And out of that relationship, and guided by a skilled practitioner, I had found the reconciliation I needed to help me move on. Something broken in me had been healed.

Kelly's story is, however, very different. Having lost her husband Jake just before his fiftieth birthday, she was devastated by his death. Life for Kelly and her family had always been difficult, as they seemed to have spent the years stumbling from one crisis to another. Jake's death was one more tragedy to cope with. However, with remarkable resilience, Kelly got on with living. She had responsibilities to fulfil. A son in and out of prison for drug-related offences was one facet of that. Trips to visit him in jail were regular and loving. Bailing him out of yet another crisis when he was on the outside was costly but necessary. And she had the younger kids, two wee ones and a teenager still at home. They needed security and stability, and that's what they got.

Of course Kelly struggled. Who wouldn't in her circumstances? She kept going out of loyalty to Jake. She wasn't going to let her kids down because of what had happened. That had always been her way. Yet the very man in whose memory she battled on was the one person on whom she had always been able to rely and from whom she could gain strength, and he wasn't around any more. So, in that paradox of learning to live again after a death, Kelly got on with things, and by any measurement did remarkably well. However, the 'missing bit', the part that pined for Jake, was never very far away. She felt she needed to see him again, to make contact. So she got in touch with a medium, and a reading was duly arranged for an evening in her own home. Kelly told me this story some months after the event, and was quite calm about it then. But she also told me that it was the first time she had told anyone, so perturbed was she by what had happened.

The technique the medium used – which I confess I hadn't heard of before – was that if Jake 'made contact' Kelly would see him in the medium's face. So she was to keep concentrating on his face so she would see her man if he was there. While she was concentrating, the medium was telling Kelly things about Jake's death that she insisted he could never have got from anyone else. Then, over a few minutes, she was convinced that the medium's face began to change. She was sure she could see Jake, and when the medium's mouth turned up slightly into a representation of Jake's cheeky grin, Kelly freaked! 'No,' she shouted, 'no more! Go away! Go away!' And the moment was gone.

Now, I have no idea what was happening there. I do not know if people can be contacted through the spirit world or if dead people can manifest themselves in a medium's face. I simply do not know if

Kelly was seeing Jake for real or whether it was her imagination fuelled by her desire. But I am very interested in her reaction. What is happening to her? She wants to see her husband, yet when it 'happens' she shouts for him to go away. 'Being demanded whether a good spirit or bad ... returned no answer.'[47] She is 'spooked' by what is taking place. So why arrange a 'reading' if you do not want to handle the outcome? It seemed to me then and it seems to me now that Kelly was simply seeking to keep open and alive the relationship with her husband. She was trying to come to terms with his 'presence' in a way she could understand. No visualisation for her, but an attempt at contact with a spirit who had passed over. But that – if the manifestation was true – was too real. And as she told me, 'If I knew I could contact him once, I know I would want more. I would want him again and again. I would have wanted him permanently. I would have needed the bloody medium to move in ...'

So, freaked-out as she had been, she never contacted the medium again. Preferring to 'keep contact' with Jake in her own way – times of tears, moments of anger, places of memory, and the occasional 'laughing out loud'. And that's what she goes on doing, in the midst of a life that still continues to be an amazing mixture of craziness and commitment.

The movie *Calendar Girls* tells the true and moving story of a widow trying to come to terms with the death of her husband, and, as one facet of that, setting up a fundraising enterprise with her friends in the Women's Institute. It takes the form of a nude – but tasteful – calendar, with the women posing nude in some of the everyday enterprises that would be familiar to all WI women. The unfolding of the story is both deeply poignant and extremely funny.

The soundtrack of the film is carefully and sensitively chosen. One track is sung by Beth Nielsen Chapman[48], and while lyrics alone cannot convey the beauty of the music and words together, they express in some fashion what all the stories in this chapter, and

elsewhere in this book, are about. For they express the deep searching for signs that the person who has died is still around, still matters
and can still be related to. You search because of the love you have
shared, and, however it is worked out, the 'finding' will be in love
too. I am grateful to Beth for her permission to print her words.

I'll catch your smile on someone's face,
Your whisper in the wind's embrace;
Through diamond stars and songs and dreams,
I find your love in everything

The sun, the sky, the rolling sea,
All conspire to comfort me;
From sorrow's edge life's beauty seems
To find your love in everything.

I've come to trust the hope it brings,
To find your love in everything;
Even as I fall apart,
Even through my shattered heart,

I'll catch your smile on someone's face...
Amazing grace.

Searching for the spirit is part of the grieving process. The searching is about the pain of the loss and the love that has mattered so
much. The searching never stops, because the loving still remains.

Notes

46   Shakespeare, *Julius Caesar*, Act III Scene iii.
47   John Aubrey (1626–1697), from *Miscellanies – Apparitions*.
48   'I Find Your Love', by Beth Nielsen Chapman/Patrick Doyle, from the
     CD *Look*, Sanctuary Records, SANCD269, included in the soundtrack
     for *Calendar Girls*.

I looked for you in every face

I looked for you in every face I saw,
I searched for you in crowded street,
I yearned to see you in my open door
To make my life complete.

But all I see are strangers' faces there,
No one to recognise as you.
And when I look, you do not come to me
As I would want you to.

I longed for you to fill your fireside chair,
I dreamed that you still shared my bed,
I listened for your footstep in the hall,
Familiar gentle tread.

But all I gaze upon is emptiness,
And every day I wake alone.
I hear no welcome sound to comfort me,
No gentle, soothing tone.

I prayed that I would feel your presence when
I cried for love to make me whole.
I craved for peace to ease my aching heart,
For healing in my soul.

But prayers are never answered in the way
I hoped. Does God not hear my plea?
I find no stillness for my raging thoughts,
No word to comfort me.

And yet, and yet I know it will be so,
Until that day will dawn, when I
Will know your presence does not then depend
On ache or painful sigh;

When I will know you in my life, my heart,
My soul, and all I'm yet to be,
When I will find you in that secret place
Where you will come to me;

When I will need no fireside chair to hold
Your spirit's presence in this place;
When gentle steps are not required to bear
Your love and blesséd grace.

When prayers need not be said to bring you back
From heaven, to fill this lonely earth;
When rage has done its worst and I've survived,
And found again my worth;

When you and I are one in love again,
In letting go and holding on;
When time has bid us glimpse eternity,
And aching days are gone.

I know that day will come when I will see
Your face, and smile again. So I
Will love you, and I'll wait with patience till
I need no longer cry –

But laugh and sing, and share our lives once more
In love that death cannot destroy.
My love, my life, my hope, my one, my all,
My everlasting joy.

You are all around

I saw you in the roses
when they bloomed in summer light.
I glimpsed in our holy place,
embraced by candle-light.
I heard you in the music,
though there was no song being sung,
And I knew that you were near me once again.

I smelt you in the perfume
of a random passer-by,
I found you in the sunset
when it filled the evening sky,
I sensed you sit beside me,
though I knew no reason why.
And I'm glad that you were near me once again.

I saw you in the footsteps
stretching far across the sand,
I felt you in the woodland
as you gently touched my hand,
I held you on the hillside,
though the moment was unplanned.
In embracing you were near me once again.

I watched you in the gentle waves
that lapped our favourite shore.
I laughed out loud though waves would drown
My voice with awesome roar.
I sensed you would be waiting
when my key unlocked my door.
And I longed to have you near me once again.

I felt you lie beside me
as I lay in restless sleep.
I heard your gentle sobbing
in the times I had to weep.
I knew you in the silence
which will still our secrets keep.
And thank God, my love, you're near me once again.

I need you when I need you,
when I love you to be near.
I love you when I love you,
in my laughing and my tears.
I miss you, and to lose you from my living is my fear,
I want you to be near me,
how I need you to be near me,
in our love you will be near me,
and, thank God, you're ever near me,
when my joy gives way to pain.
Yes, my love, you're here, so near me, once again.

My love

Quietly,
gently,
you come to me,
touching,
holding,
it has to be;
smiling,
whispering,
you stay with me,
my love.

Weeping,
screaming,
I felt you go,
hoping,
praying
it was not so;
yearning,
cursing,
I let you go,
my love.

Meaning,
knowing
you are with me;
memories,
always
you still must be;
dreaming,
keeping,
at one with me,
my love

Twelve

Lost saints

'I love thee with a love I seemed to lose
With my lost saints, — I love thee with the breath,
Smiles, tears, of all my life ! — and, if God choose,
I shall but love thee better after death.'
Elizabeth Barrett Browning: 'How can I love thee? Let me count
the ways.'

'Requiem aeternam dona eis, Domine: et lux perpetua luceat eis.'
(Grant them eternal rest, O Lord; and let perpetual light shine upon them.)
The Mass in Latin

I was asked recently to read Elizabeth Barrett Browning's lovely
words, 'How can I love thee, let me count the ways', at the funeral
service of a young man. They had been chosen by his wife as an
expression of their love together. The words had been read at their
wedding two years before and were, she told me, as true in death as
they were in life. I had neither read nor heard these words before.
They have since become very precious.

I love thee to the depth and breadth and height
My soul can reach, when feeling out of sight
For the ends of Being and ideal Grace.
I love thee to the level of everyday's
Most quiet need, by sun and candle-light.
I love thee freely, as men strive for Right;
I love thee purely, as they turn from Praise.
I love thee with the passion put to use
In my old griefs, and with my childhood's faith.
I love thee with a love I seemed to lose

With my lost saints, — I love thee with the breath,
Smiles, tears, of all my life! — and, if God choose,
I shall but love thee better after death.

These beautiful words speak so eloquently of a love shared, in all its facets, between two people. No wonder it was read at a wedding. No wonder it was asked for at a funeral service. For it speaks of a love that not even death can threaten. Whether 'I shall but love thee better after death' means that the love shared will be deepened in bereavement or continued in a better form when the couple are reunited after they have died is open to interpretation. But however it is understood, it expresses a hope that after a death love will continue in a deeper and better form.

For the Christian, and indeed for all those whose religious beliefs give them the security of a concept of an 'afterlife', the interpretation of 'after death' would point to a heaven, a place of meeting again on 'the other side'. Such a concept, if it is held in faith, can give those who grieve a hope that sustains them in bereavement. Faith in a life after death, with a love shared that is even better than we have known in this world, is the lifeline that is crucially important to many in their journey of loss. Even those who say, 'I'm not sure there's a heaven,' still have hopes, and these hopes can and do sustain them in their bereavement.

However, not all Christians find that their faith gives them the framework they need in their loss, and for some it may even serve to confuse the grief process. There are many reasons why this might be so. Geoff Walters's book, *Why Do Christians Find it Hard to Grieve?*, which I have mentioned in an earlier chapter, gives many useful insights into this issue. And there are numerous suggestions as to how it might be tackled. This chapter explores one such suggestion: working towards a renewed understanding of the communion of saints. This concept has the potential to allow Christians to grieve in a healthy way, while still holding to principles and beliefs informed by their faith. Browning's suggestion is that we seem to lose our love with our 'lost saints'. To find these lost saints again may, therefore, allow us to hear some reassurance about our bereavement journey, and may indeed enable us to find and know love again.

Jessie was a devoutly Christian woman, a regular worshipper at her church, with a supportive faith community and a helpful pastor. Jessie missed her husband more than she could say. She cried openly when she talked about her loss. She was struggling without her partner, her constant companion and her best friend. In the midst of tears in one of our bereavement support groups I remember Jessie sharing this with us. 'I'm so sorry. I shouldn't be crying like this. My faith is strong. I know John's safe with God. I know we'll meet again some day. So why am I so sad? I shouldn't be like this. I shouldn't be upset if my Christian faith means so much to me.'

The anguish expressed by Jessie, exacerbated by the faith dimension of her life, is not at all uncommon. It would be wrong to say that Christians cope less well with loss than those who have no faith, but in my experience of hospice chaplaincy and bereavement support there are elements of the Christian perspective which contrive to slow down or disrupt the grieving process. Of course it is clear that spiritual belief has a positive effect on the resolution of bereavement. People who profess stronger spiritual beliefs seem to resolve their grief more rapidly and completely after a death than do people with no spiritual beliefs. A framework of faith can be a healing environment which well supports the bereavement process. More specifically, a belief in an 'afterlife', combined with other elements of faith, gives people a framework of hope and purpose that assists them with end-of-life issues and the dying process. And, in bereavement, it helps alleviate their sense of loss and separation from a loved one.

Walter Scott writes[49]:

Love rules the court, the camp, the grove,
And men below, and saints above;
For love is heaven, and heaven is love.

With 'men below and saints above', we have our glimpse of
heaven, we hold to our faith, we have a perspective on things that
work for us, even in tragedy, and we are sustained in our loss. Love
rules, even in death. However this is not a universal assurance for all
religious people. For many, the faith which they expect to be of help
and support, and which they lean on for meaning and purpose when
they need it most, doesn't work as they expect it to. And, sadly, for
some it actually has a counterproductive effect.

In recent times we have all been affected by tragedies which,
though specific to one area and culture, are so graphic and all-
consuming that they have an impact on people far and wide. The
tragedy of the Twin Towers on 11th September 2001 is one of those.
The tsunami in the Indian Ocean on Boxing Day of 2004 is another.
Amidst all the aftermath of such events there are the inevitable questions about where God is in all of this. Not surprisingly there are
stories of some people who were personally affected by one of these
traumas whose cherished beliefs were so challenged by the hell of
their experience that they lost or abandoned their faith altogether.
And you and I know that it need not take such major events as these
to challenge or shatter deeply held beliefs and a faith perspective.
How many times have we heard, as someone has related to us their
own life trauma: 'I used to believe, but I lost my faith over this.'

As a consequence, work with religious people who are bereaved
asks of professionals and carers not only an understanding of their
grief, but also an engagement with those elements of faith, or loss of
faith, that add to the confusion and the pain of the bereavement
journey. For example, Christians in loss are expected to be sustained
by the belief – indeed, the certainty – that the person who has died

rests in the nearer presence of God, So, we tend to think that they should be so uplifted by the prospect of eventually being reunited with their loved one that they need not grieve for the loss. 'And, if God choose, I shall but love thee better after death'.

This, sadly and ultimately destructively, can lead to the denial of true feelings, and a dismissal of the brokenness and devastation that is a natural part of the grieving process. For some Christians the concept of the immortality of the soul and eternal rest sustains them in their grief. But for others, equally committed to their faith, it serves to create a tension between what they feel is expected of them – witnessing to their faith, being an example to others, being strong because of the sustaining presence of God, and the like – and true, human feelings – hopelessness, emptiness, deep sorrow, confusion, doubt, despair, tears, etc which are the natural responses to loss. Such was Jessie's tension in her grieving for her husband. Indeed, within that tension there may even have been an element of the suppressed anger so commonly found among those who will not allow themselves to be openly bitter against the God of Love in whom they have always believed.

The Bible doesn't always help! Words like those of St Paul – 'We do not want you to grieve like the rest of men who have no hope'[50] – give signals that faith should make us strong, when at the same time we feel the brokenness of our loss. What is needed is to feel the pain of the loss and to work through the grief before there can be any wholehearted embracing of the hope of new beginnings. Jessie felt that tears were inconsistent with her faith. She was letting the side down, and letting God down too. Faith in God and her grieving didn't go together.

Yet the feelings grief brings are not the antithesis of faith. Grieving is not some kind of religious failure, nor an indication of a lack of commitment or belief. The natural, human responses to loss are integral to any faith system we might have, and our beliefs should not suppress but rather embrace our real human feelings. Jessie needed release from her despair. She did not need a release from her deep feelings of loss, for she had to understand them and accept them and see them for what they were: appropriate grief reactions. But she needed to be freed from the tensions, the unhelpful tensions, which her Christian faith was creating for her.

Good bereavement support affirms the realities and rightness of feelings, emotions and the turmoil of bereavement. Grief reactions, regardless of one's life or faith perspective, should be seen not only as understandable and acceptable, but also as vitally important in the journey of loss, to be worked through in a healthy and honest way. Grief brings with it many emotions, fears and anxieties, all of which are associated with the facing of mortality. Such feelings are natural and healthy, and have to be recognised as such by bereaved people and the professionals whose support they seek.

Sadly, people in loss are all too readily and neatly 'labelled', causing the professional carer to feel that their behaviour and feelings can be defined and measured at any given moment in time. This only serves to put further pressure on the bereaved person. They are made to feel that if they haven't moved on to the 'next stage' within a given time-frame, then they have somehow failed or are stuck or there is something wrong with them. In addition, many in the caring professions still view grief and loss as something from which to recover or move on rather than a process or journey to be worked through. In a society which itself is impatient and rushes from one thing to another, bereaved people are too often given only a very limited time to express the public aspects of their grief. This serves to increase the isolation people feel over time in their loss, and decreases the likelihood that their feelings will be accepted and their time-frame and behaviour patterns individualised.

There is sometimes an unfortunate belief that the 'stages of grief' model can be a 'one size fits all' approach. This creates a focus on abnormalities, and extremes are seen as unhealthy. While this might be a tidy way for many professionals to label bereaved people so that they feel they can respond accordingly, it further isolates the bereaved in their grief and pathologises or 'medicalises' rather than normalises their reactions.

Take Cathy, for example. Cathy had been inseparable from her widowed mother, having lived with her all her life. The house was empty without her. Life had little purpose or meaning. 'The only thing that gives me comfort,' she confessed, 'is feeling my mother around me. I wear her favourite cardigan when I sit by the fire. And sometimes I even hear her voice. My friend tells me I'm loopy, but I don't think so. Do you?' Cathy was, in the framework of the previous chapter, searching for the spirit of her mother, for she needed to continue to relate to her mother even though she was dead. No, of course she wasn't loopy. But because she was struggling to understand what was happening, these strange feelings or behaviour patterns might suggest to her, or to someone else, that she was on the brink of madness. Yet Cathy was simply working through a process of relating to her mother in a new way. In what was for her very natural behaviour, Cathy was in effect questioning the assumption that the grief process needs to be completed, either in stages or at a definable end point, and that bereaved people need to show clear signs of 'moving on'. She was simply working through a continuing relationship. She was doing what came naturally, accepting the devastation of the death as well as working out how she might remain close to her mother. That's what was being symbolised by Cathy and her mother's cardigan.

What, then, does this have to offer to the Christian who finds it hard to grieve? Perhaps Terry can give us a clue. In his own way, Terry was coming to terms with the same thing. 'My father was no saint,' he told me, 'not in the way he lived, anyway, and not in any measurement of the saints you hear about in churches or see in stained-glass windows. But though he's been dead a long time, he's still as important to me as he ever was. In fact, I can feel his influence more than ever. I suppose that kind of makes him a saint for me, don't you think?' What Terry was working out in his continued relationship with his father was something to do with 'The Communion of Saints'. Such a concept, enshrined in Christian thinking but also sitting naturally with the continued relationships we all see in loss, indicates that we remain inextricably linked with those who have died. It holds in one concept the reality of death, the pain of loss and separation, and the continuing union with and influence of those who have 'gone before'. It offers us our personal communion of saints, with whom, in both human relationships and in the theological concept of the oneness of the Faithful, we remain inextricably bound.

I have unfolded the importance of this in the bereavement journey, for Christian and non-Christian alike, in the chapter in *A Need For Living* devoted to this issue, so I won't rehearse it again in detail here. But in short, the image used, of our saints being those who sit with us around our table, with whom we continue to 'commune' and who continue to influence us in their living as well as in their dying, is the concept of sainthood which Terry had grasped so readily and rightly in the continuing bond with his long-deceased father. In human terms, we are greatly influenced by a limited number of people – close family, good friends, and the like – with whom we interact throughout our lives, but we are also touched by people of whom we have read, people whose writings, poetry, music have influenced us, or who, in their exploits and influence in their day, continue to affect our lives many generations later. These are the ones who sit around our table, with whom we talk, to whom we listen, from whom we gain wisdom, as we make decisions and formulate attitudes in our daily living. They are, in effect, our saints, the people who matter most to us. And such is their influence, and such is their continued importance to us, that when they die, their seat at the table does not become empty. It is not vacated to be filled by someone else, but remains occupied as they remain with us, integral to our lives, even though we are separated from them by death. This concept of the Communion of Saints, properly understood and effectively used, can give Christians that which they most need: an acceptance of both sides of the bereavement coin – the pain of the loss, and continued connectedness with the departed. Indeed, it can also offer those who have no belief in an afterlife the same reassurance that their own saints are still very, very important to them.

We can help those people with a religious or specific Christian perspective to regain their equilibrium after a loss and during their bereavement journey. We have to begin by helping them see that grief and expressions of sorrow and devastation in their loss are real and healthy and should not and need not be suppressed by faith or the behavioural expectations of those who live by such a faith. We have the task of reinterpreting our theology of death, so that the pain and 'hellishness' of loss is seen as integral to faith and not the antithesis of it. And if we hold to and understand a workable concept of the Communion of Saints, we can create a healthy combination of the personal experiences of loss, current theories in which these experiences make sense, and a theology that continues to offer hope, thus allowing the Christian to grieve in a healthy and honest way.

And Jessie? Well, she never really learned to be comfortable with her tears. Cathy? She still misses her mother and feels her very near, but doesn't need her cardigan so much now to make it so. And Terry? Well, his dad is still a saint, and will always be, and 'love is heaven and heaven is love' for them both.

I have been a member of the Iona Community since 1973, and my wife since 1983. Mary and I met and fell in love on Iona, and for us individually and together Iona has been our spiritual home and the Iona Community a constantly sustaining framework for life and faith. There are many facets to the work of the Iona Community and its presence on Iona that are stimulating and challenging, and of course these mean different things at different times. But in the context of this book, and in particular the theme of this chapter, I highlight one issue which is of special importance to me.

Members of the Iona Community have a commitment to pray regularly for one another in a monthly cycle. On the 31st day of the month, and printed along with all the members in our booklet of members, there are the names of those members of the Iona Community who have died. It's a kind of monthly remembrance of those who are no longer with us, and not only does the list get longer as the years pass but every year there are more names included in it of people I have actually known. So I put this marker down now – I hope the Iona Community never discontinues the practice of remembering its saints on a regular basis. I don't want these saints to be lost. I want to pray for them and remember them and commune with them as often as I can. And, one day, I'd be happy to be remembered in this way too!

I close this chapter, therefore, by sharing a reading by Erik Cramb and a short prayer by Joy Mead, both included in *This Is the Day*,[51] a book of readings and prayers which parallels the monthly prayer cycle of the Iona Community. They are to be read in conjunction with the 'saints' remembered on the 31st day of the month. I offer them without comment, for their words and meaning speak power-fully enough for themselves.

In the midst of death there is life (Revelation 21:1–4)

It is hard to imagine that there is anything much worse in our experience today than to endure the agony and the impotence of watching someone we love withering away, devoured before our very eyes by a cancer we are power-less to combat. Recently I was called to conduct the funeral of a man of 65 years of age, Harry by name, the last two years of whose life had been spent in the increasingly unequal struggle against cancer, and who had for most of these two years been nursed at home gently and devoutly by his wife, Jean. In preparation for the funeral I had spent an evening sitting chatting to the new widow, getting from her a flavour of the 47 years of married life they had shared. She told me the story of their teenage romance; how, when they were married, he was only 19, an apprentice in the Yards; she, just a messenger girl. How married life had begun in a room in her in-laws' home; how they lost a son as a little child; how their other son had thrived, and grown and prospered and had given her and her husband the joy of being grandparents. How her husband had loved his work (he worked in the shipyards all his days), how he had been 'a good Union man'; how he had enjoyed the simple pleasures of a pint and a wee flutter on a Saturday; how he liked to watch the Rangers, and in his later years watch the snooker on TV. He was also a Mason and in the Orange Lodge, but a quiet, decent man who held no truck with the more aggressive expressions of some of his brothers. Most of all she said, 'Though he was no saint, none of us are, he was a good man and a good father. They told me I was daft getting married at 17, but they were wrong. I'd do it all over again if I got the chance.' Harry's funeral took place on a Saturday morning and was one of those 'good' funerals where thanksgiving is genuine, where the dignity and the worth of the deceased was evident to all; where mourning, though real, was quietly cushioned by the hope of the Resurrection. After the funeral service Jean asked me if I was taking my boy to see the Thistle that afternoon. I told her no I wasn't, for I had a wedding to do at three o'clock. 'A wedding,' she said with a sigh. 'Aw, that's nice.' Then, after seeming to think about it for a while she said, 'Would you tell the bride I wish her all the best, and tell her if she's half as lucky as me, she'll be all right.' So, at the wedding service I told the young bride of the old widow and her wishes for her. The bride cried and afterwards said she just couldn't imagine a nicer greeting on her wedding day. Then she asked if I would take her bouquet after the wedding up to the widow. This I was delighted to do. Then it was Jean's turn to shed a tear of joy. The bride and the widow, joined together in the shared joy of love. Even though they never met, they made each other's day.

Elemental

When my time is over
and fire has consumed
all flesh, take my dust
and scatter it
where you can feel
earth, water, rushing air
that I may be
whole.

Then take away with you
memories, burning in fire,
fresh as air, rolling as the sea,
still as the earth
and this shall be
my resurrection.

Notes

[49] Sir Walter Scott (1771–1832), from 'Love'.

[50] Thessalonians 4:13.

[51] *This Is the Day*, ed. Neil Paynter, Wild Goose Publications, ISBN 1901557634.

Saints and sinners?

He was my saint,
My light,
The wind beneath my wings;
He was my life,
My all,
Sustainer of those things
That made me ever blessed
By saintly love.

He was no saint –
No light
Held up to guide his path;
A sinner, he,
But real –
For in his heart was truth
That made me often blessed
By saintly love.

You are my saint,
My light
To shine; to guide the way
For those who come
Behind
Upon this road; to pray
That they are being blessed
By saints like you.

You are no saint –
Yet light
Shines from your life, so we,
Whom you have loved
With all
You have and are, can see

More sinners are being blessed
As saints are too.

We too are saints –
A light
In every sinner's hand,
To hold up high,
And show,
Ev'n in a life unplanned,
That even we are blessed
With saintly skill.

So sinners, too,
Are saints –
Though in a different guise;
They are our truth,
So real,
Ev'n though in others' eyes
They've never known they're blessed,
And never will.

Too small a saint

I'm far too small a saint
Than I would want to be.
I've been too big a sinner
Once again.

So use this little saint –
It's all that I can be –
In place of me the sinner,
Please! Amen

Who will remember?

When sympathies have all been said, and kind words been expressed;
when funeral crowds have come and gone and paid their last respects;
when no more cards come in the post, and phones ring less and less –
who will remember then?

When birthdays come and go and still no silly card's been bought;
when holiday brochures are binned without a passing thought;
when each choice is another lonely battle to be fought –
who will remember then?

When year has followed year and I'm expected to behave;
when every weeping movie has me standing at your grave;
when even friends stop commenting on how I am so brave –
who will remember then?

When everyone's decided to stop mentioning your name;
when people try to use me in their socialising game;
when every day seems empty and each empty day's the same –
who will remember then?

Will you care for me when caring's out of date, and care some more;
will you talk with me when talking brings the same tears as before;
will you wait with me when waiting takes too long, and is too sore –
will you remember then?

Thirteen

New journeys now begin

'There must be a beginning of any great matter, but the continuing unto the end until it be thoroughly finished yields the true glory'
Sir Francis Drake

'It is impossible that anything so natural, so necessary and so universal as death should ever have been designed by Providence as an evil to mankind'
Jonathan Swift

I want to offer this penultimate chapter as a positive note. And I can think of no better way of doing so than to tell you the story of Sue and Hamish. I have asked their permission to tell their story, and though they are embarrassed that it would ever appear in print, I am delighted that they have allowed me to share it with you.

Sue's husband, Steve, and Hamish's wife, Sheila, were patients in our hospice round about the same time. They were in different wards and being cared for by different staff. As families came and went to visit, including Sue and Hamish, they would no doubt be aware of other visitors coming and going to see other people. But there had been no need and no opportunity for them to meet or be aware of each other. They were focused on their own purposes, and even in a busy hospice wouldn't have noticed much about anyone else.

Both couples were in similar circumstances. There were no children and all four of them were of an age – late forties/early fifties. The support for their respective partners was tender and loving. And the process of facing a death was a heavy burden to carry. In time, Sue and Hamish had to face their respective losses, a few weeks apart as I recall, and in time (eight to twelve weeks after the date of the bereavement, as is the practice in our bereavement support system) both were invited to our support groups. I have said a little about our hospice's bereavement support system earlier in this book, but perhaps a word or two of further explanation would be useful here.

When people are invited to our sessions, we ask them to let us know if they intend to come. Consequently, in preparation for our monthly group meetings, and being aware of who is coming, we set up small groups so that these bereaved people can meet and share with each other. Each group has a trained group facilitator, and we make up the groups so that, as far as is possible, those attending meet with people with whom they will have something in common. There may be a group of five older partners, for example, another with a mother and daughter with a mother and son, one of four siblings, and another with five younger partners, and so on. What we don't do is to have everyone in the group at the same stage of their loss, particularly in the early stages. Later on, when people may have got to know each other and a number may be coming up to the anniversary of their bereavement, for example, being in a group with those you have already shared with may be helpful. But, at the start, people are just too raw and are hurting too much to have all the emotion of the start of the bereavement journey in the one group. So, the groups will usually contain individuals at different stages of their loss, and in sharing and listening, in understanding and support-ing one another, they learn from each other, feel less isolated in their grief, and can begin to accept and understand their feelings and reac-tions to their loss.

Given that people grieve at varying rates and have different and unfolding needs, those who come to the groups are invited to come back month by month up to the anniversary of the death. Some come once or twice, some for a few months, and some for the full year. And if they do come regularly, they will meet with different individuals in different groups, and the group leaders will change around too. Sometimes they will be with people they know, and sometimes they will be meeting new people, but always sharing, listening and learning, and hopefully in groups that are always open and beneficial.

Such was the case for Sue and Hamish. At that time we had a number of younger partners attending, and, though new people came and went over the months, quite naturally Sue and Hamish found themselves in the same group from time to time. They, and a number of the others, lived near each other or worked in the same location. And we were aware of phone numbers being exchanged, meetings for coffee being arranged, and the like, among a number of the participants – something, indeed, we are keen to encourage and which is not at all uncommon. Our groups only happen monthly. People have bereavement needs all the time. So, meeting together, sharing the journey and finding ongoing support is always helpful.

In time, in the autumn of that year, both Sue and Hamish came to the end of their time with us in our bereavement support system. Delightful people, they had both done well in their journey of loss and had been supportive of each other and those with whom they had shared over the months. We knew that they, with some of the others, were committed to keeping in touch with each other as well as with the hospice as time went on, and were now ready to face the future with their own strength and purpose. There we expected the story to end. But not so ...

In the spring of the following year I got a phone call at work from Sue. That wasn't uncommon of itself, for Sue – as with others over the years – would phone from time to time to check something out, to mark an anniversary, to hear a reassuring word, to ask for advice, or just to keep in touch. But this time it was different. She asked if she could meet me, but not at the hospice, somewhere on our own, nice and quiet. Indeed, could she come to see me after work – that day! So, an arrangement was made that she would collect me later from work and we would go for a coffee. I have to admit that I was intrigued and not a little worried. Had things gone wrong? Was there a crisis we hadn't anticipated? Was this going to be a difficult meeting? Should I really be seeing her away from the hospice environs? These and other questions were buzzing around my head when she picked me up at 5 o'clock and we drove into town. We chit-chatted about this and that and it was clear that no real distress was evident. So what could it be?

We got to the pub down the road, ordered coffee, and Sue and I sat together (side by side, I recall, with no eye contact possible. Bad move, as it turned out!). When we were done with the 'Do you take sugar?' and 'Would you like a biscuit' stuff, Sue sat quietly for a moment, and then she said, 'There's something I want to tell you.' 'Yes,' I responded. 'It's about Hamish!' 'Uh huh?' 'We've been seeing each other.' 'Yes, I know that – coffee and things.' *(Funny thing to take me out to tell me when I know that already …)* 'No, there's more than that. We've been *seeing* each other!' *(Oh, how do I get him to understand?)* 'Uh huh!' *(It's very strange, all of this …)* '*SEEING* each other, the two of us, like … going out … together … Hamish and me …' *(Oh God, how can I make it any clearer?)* 'Yes, I know … Oh. OH! … You mean seeing … *(My God, does she mean what I think she means?)* You … and Hamish … like … SEEING … Oh wow! Sue, that's wonderful!'

If people can leap up and down while sitting still in a public place, then that's what Sue and I did together. I held her hand and squeezed it tightly. I think I bounced in my seat. I turned to look at her. She was crying gently. I'd seen her cry many times before, but not like this. For now she was smiling as well. And I was smiling too, the biggest smile you could ever imagine. What the people around us thought, we didn't care. It was one of the happiest moments I can remember.

When we had composed ourselves and I turned towards her to look at her face as she was speaking (if I'd done that before I might have picked up the signals earlier!) Sue told me her story. It had been just before Christmas, and she had decided, fifteen months after her husband had died and facing the second Christmas of her bereavement, that she would make the effort and put up a Christmas tree. So the artificial tree with its different sections was unearthed and she had attempted to put it together. But it wouldn't fit. Try as she would, she couldn't get the tree in place. It was all going wrong, a complete disaster. She needed help. She needed someone who would understand. So, with tears in her eyes, she had phoned Hamish, someone, anyone who would know what she was going through and who would be patient with her in her silliness – and hopefully get the tree up! Hamish, thankfully, was at home. And hearing of Sue's dilemma and sadness offered to come round right away. So, he had come to her house, found Sue in tears, and gathered her up in a great big hug. And at that moment, Sue told me, 'something happened'! This wasn't just a friendly hug. This was special.

Neither of them was really sure what was happening. But both of them knew that they felt very good indeed. In time, the tree was put up, but that was the least of it. A relationship had begun, or an established relationship of friendship had taken a different and unexpected turn. The long and the short of it was that they had fallen in love.

As you might expect, Sue and Hamish were tentative and careful at first, not wanting to rush at anything and make a mistake. But they were in love, and love had given them a new beginning that they had neither looked for nor expected. To cut a long story short, Hamish and Sue got engaged and were married just over a year later. In the wonderful surroundings of the Library of the Royal College of Physicians in Edinburgh, their lovely, tender relationship and their new beginning was confirmed in their marriage. I had the enormous pleasure of conducting the wedding ceremony. Colleagues from the hospice bereavement support team were there. Bereaved relatives with whom Hamish and Sue had shared some of their journey of loss were also valued guests. And, of course, both Hamish and Sue's families were there to celebrate their new beginning.

But it was another facet of the wedding celebration which fascinated and encouraged me even more. When I had gone to Sue and Hamish's home to prepare the wedding with them, we sat together in a lovely front room. And there, on the baby-grand piano (a gift from and to each other to celebrate their new beginning), on the mantelpiece and on the sideboard there were lots of photographs. There were pictures of Sue and Steve, of Hamish and Sheila, and of Sue and Hamish, all mixed up together, one beside the other, a whole gallery of loves past and present. I remarked on that at the time, did so again in the wedding service, and have commented on it many times since. For it is a real symbol, a parable if you like, of the grief process. In a very real sense Sue still loves Steve and Hamish still loves Sheila. These two loving partners and the times shared and enjoyed are fully part of their lives, and will always remain so. They take these relationships into their new beginning. They acknowledge, with each other and for themselves, the whole of their journey of life. They had shared that in our bereavement groups. They know that is part of their love for each other. They will continue to affirm it as their 'new journeys now begin'.

So, present at the wedding service, and continuing that powerful symbol, were members of Sheila and Steve's families. For they too were happy for Sue and Hamish, and as they were part of their past they would be part of their future too. 'New journeys now begin' for them as well. Very touchingly, Hamish and Sue asked me in the opening prayer in the marriage service – the prayer that offers thanks for all that has brought a couple to their wedding day – to give thanks for Sheila and Steve, and the loves and journeys that had been shared with them. If ever there was an example of 'continuing bonds' and 'new journeys' all intertwined, then it was in that moment of thanksgiving.

Sue and Hamish have put theory into practice for me. And while not everyone gets remarried after a death or would ever want to, and not everyone has the opportunity to exhibit such a public symbol of a new beginning, these lovely people give me hope that things will and do come right. Hamish and Sue have both taken early retirement and are blissfully happy together. They still have photographs of Sheila and Steve in their front room, and more recent pictures of happy times that they have experienced together. Life began again for them, and begins again every day – hope for them and hope for us all!

Sue and Hamish knew that 'there must be a beginning of any great matter, but the continuing unto the end until it be thoroughly finished yields the true glory'[52]. They had continued to the end, and had found their own glory. But they also knew where they had begun, at the despair of loss. Despair is a common and understandable emotion at the commencement of the journey of grief. This prayer from the sensitive writings of the late Kate McIlhagga, from *Praying for the Dawn: A resource book for the ministry of healing*[53], expresses the nature of that despair all too well:

Despair is a desperate companion
for facing the unknown.
Much rather the funny, dancing
loving partner of my journey,
the spirit of sparkling hope
to lighten my load
and wash away my tears.
Perhaps I'm searching in the wrong place;
asking the wrong questions.
O God, midwife of my life,
deliver me from my anxiety,
dispel my fear,
calm my racing heart,
bring hope to birth again.

Both Hamish and Sue had lived with that despair. We knew that in our bereavement support groups, for we had heard them talk openly and honestly about their struggles with bereavement often enough. I remember Hamish telling us of a time when he broke down peeling potatoes of all things, because he had had this sudden and overwhelming memory of the times when Sheila had stood beside him sharing that mundane chore. Yes indeed, he and Sue knew what despair was about. But hope had also come to birth for them. Who knows who or what their midwife was? Who knows what the process was of helping them move from despair to hope? But there is no doubting that hope came alive and they were delivered, 'born again', into a new beginning.

Jonathan Swift wrote, 'It is impossible that anything so natural, so necessary and so universal as death should ever have been designed by Providence as an evil to mankind.'[54] Death comes to us all. It is natural and necessary. It is not evil. Bereavement is common to the human condition. It cannot be designed to destroy us. So, just as despair is right and real, so hope has to be there too. When we recall Eric Bogle's words,

Without joy, there is no grief;
Without hope, there's no belief;
Without love, Death's just a thief
Who steals nothing more than time.

we know again that without hope, there can be no belief in a future. So in our losses we are sustained by the hope of a new beginning. We don't know what form it will take, but we will surely know it when it happens. The example of an unfolding future that is Sue and Hamish's story is there to sustain us.

When Henry VIII asked Miles Coverdale to produce an English translation of the Bible, Coverdale knew very well his own limitations and his lack of the necessary scholarship in Hebrew and Greek.

'Considering how excellent knowledge and learning an interpreter of scripture ought to have in the tongues, and pondering also mine own insufficiency therein, and how weak I am to perform the office of translator, I was the more loath to meddle with this work.' But then he goes on: 'But to say the truth before God, it was neither my labour nor desire to have this work put in my hand; nevertheless it grieved me that other nations should be more plenteously provided for with the scripture in their mother tongue than we; therefore when I was instantly required, though I could not do as well as I would, I thought it my duty to do my best, and that with a good will.'

There is not one of us adequately equipped to deal with loss. Each of us, in our own circumstances, with our own grief and on our own journey, has Coverdale's 'insufficiency' and we know our own limitations only too well. And, in truth, we too would be 'loath to meddle with this work', such is our resentment at having to face loss in the first place. Yet, what are we to do? Give up the task, or do our best with it?

I wonder, sometimes, if people are encouraged by our society to make too much of their grief. It is, perhaps, because death has been 'sanitised' and pushed into the hands of professionals, leaving us with little or no personal experience of it, that we react so strongly and so deeply when bereavement comes our way. And it is certainly because we live increasingly compartmentalised lives, isolated from each other in the depth of our life experiences, that we have no norms against which to check things out, and little 'modelling' of grief reactions against which to measure our own feelings and actions. We are well enough aware of our own 'insufficiency'.

My grandmother, born in 1896, was one of 11 children, all brought into family life in a room-and-kitchen in Glasgow. Four of them died in infancy and in the house with my granny present. Her youngest brother, who lived to the ripe old age of 76, had worked in the Pit and had been a drummer in a pipe-band. Yet he had always been known as the 'weaklin' o' the family'. For Alex had been still-born, and had been revived by pouring the contents of a bottle of whisky over him. (True story, folks, for my granny was there!) It wasn't that life was cheap for my granny, or that she or her family didn't know about grief. It was just that, with death as part of living, they saw their reactions to all its horror and devastation for what they were, a normal part of how you were expected to behave, with normal feelings of loss.

I heard an Irish doctor a while ago tell of research she had done into the cultural norms of dealing with death in the Gaelic-speaking communities of Ireland and Scotland in the early part of the 20th century. And she told a story that had been shared with her by an old man, about an experience in his childhood. There had been an old man in his village who always sat at the door of his croft. Every day when the wee boy was on his way back from school he would sit with other children at the old man's feet for a while and listen to yet another fascinating story about 'the old days' before he continued on his own way home.

One day, the old man wasn't there. Back in his own home, he asked his father where the old man was. Without a word, his father took him by the hand and they walked together to the old man's croft. Inside there were many people, but weaving through them the boy and his father came upon the bedroom of the croft. And there, on the bed, dressed in his best clothes, was the old man, lying still, as if sound asleep. The wee boy was fascinated, for he had never seen the old man like this, and never with his eyes closed, and never so pale. Still holding him by the hand, his father took him over to the bed where the old man lay. Coming close, he took the wee boy's hand and laid it on the old man's cold brow. 'Donald is dead,' said his father, 'and now you will never be afraid of death again.' The wee boy, who was now his own old man, told the researcher that his father had been quite right, for death had never held any fear for him from that moment on.

I would not argue that we go back to the old days. Nor would I argue that we cease to protect people from some of the horrors of death and the waste of life. But I would argue for more understanding, and, as a result, for more 'modelling' of the grief process, so that people know and comprehend what is happening to them and are better able to cope with their feelings and reactions. It worries me a lot that when there is a tragedy or a trauma that affects a lot of people, including members of the caring professions and emergency services, we hear that 'counselling is available'. For with those words we are inclined to feel what I suspect we are supposed to feel, that this will mean that everything is now OK. We hand the grief process over to the experts. Society has done its job. Counselling is available. All is well!

Well, for some people, some of the time, it may be. But for many people a lot of the time, it simply allows us to abrogate our responsibilities for an understanding of grief and loss, pushes further away the feelings and reactions of grief into a private or professional world, and cuts needy people off from any helpful modelling of feelings that might be useful to us all. Sue and Hamish had to feel the pain and share the journey of despair before any new beginning was possible. I strongly suspect that it was that sharing that gave them the platform for a new understanding of the journey of loss and of the feelings of love for each other.

Let me close this chapter on hopefulness by offering you one last story. It's a story I recall, and need to recall, when I am in danger of having too high an opinion of myself; when, if you like, I start to feel that my professional skills and understanding are always what people need. And it reminds me that people learn to live through loss. They develop their own coping strategies, which often leave me with disbelief and wonder.

Nellie was an old woman whom I knew in my parish when I was

a young minister. She was the matriarchal head of an extensive criminal family, but was herself a real character whom I'd come to like a lot. Nellie had three deaths in her family in three weeks. Her husband dropped dead of a heart attack, her eldest son died following a diabetic coma, and her sister-in-law died a few weeks after a massive stroke. I had conducted the funerals of her husband and son, on each occasion with at least three prison cars with warders in attendance escorting various family members from HM penal institutions throughout the country – and handcuffed as well. And I had heard from family members the account of Nellie's sister-in-law's cremation.

Not surprisingly, I was concerned about the old lady's welfare, for notwithstanding the nature of people's lives they have deep feelings, and tragedy and trauma affects everyone regardless of culture, background or family circumstances. So one evening I popped round to see her. I found her at home, sitting alone by a roaring fire, looking very forlorn, and sounding very wistful. I offered her a cigarette, and, because it was close to the time I was to stop smoking altogether, my smokes were 'extra mild'. She took a cigarette, looked at it carefully, saw that it was 'extra mild', muttered, 'God, son, ye canna taste them …', broke the tip off the cigarette and threw it in the fire, lit up the now 'plain' cigarette, took a long draw from it, and said, 'But ah'll tak' yin frae you, son, fur auld time's sake, an' fur whit ye've dun fur me an' ma faimlie. God bless ye.' I could have bottled the moment and taken it home. It was such a wonderful affirmation of what we had shared together.

However, in the context of grief and loss, it was a comment later in the conversation that I remember even more. We talked a bit about how the family were coping and how Nellie herself was managing. I was amazed at her resilience. This wasn't pretence. This wasn't the cheapness of life. This wasn't a woman bemoaning her loss. This was simply old Nellie telling her story as it was, looking for no heavy sympathy nor clever counselling as a response. Maybe it was because she had learned to cope with tragedies over many years, or maybe it was because feelings of loss had been well worked through and understood. I don't know. It wasn't worth analysing too much. So I told her I was amazed at her resilience, and was encouraged by how she was able to cope. And I asked her, 'How do you manage, Nellie? How are you able to keep going through all of this?' And she replied, 'Weel, son, whit can ye dae. Ye live, ye live, and ye die, ye die. An' that's just the way it is.'

You live, you live; and you die, you die. There was no cheapness in that, and no denial of feelings. But there was an earthy reality and a basic philosophy that underpinned it. Death was part of life, and living with loss was living with what was given as part of life. Death is the given. 'That's just the way it is.' There is no escape from its reality. So, what can you do but to 'get on with it', to live through the pain and be guided by hope, to know that feelings are real but that new journeys are always possible too.

God bless you too, Nellie. You gave a young minister much-needed reassurance that while we know that 'in the midst of life there is death', we can also say with you, 'In the face of death there is life and hope.'

Notes

[52]   Sir Frances Drake (1540–1596), from a Dispatch to Sir Francis Walsingham, 17 May 1587.

[53]   *Praying for the Dawn*, ed. Ruth Burgess and Kathy Galloway, Wild Goose Publications, ISBN 190155726X.

[54]   Jonathan Swift (1667–1745), from *Thoughts on Religion*.

The logo of Marie Curie Cancer Care is the daffodil. No one has been able to explain to me when or where or by whom the choice of the daffodil was made. But it was a good choice, and the 'Fields of Hope' which Marie Curie fundraising has created throughout the country are just that — signs of hope when the daffodils burst forth in the Spring. This poem was born out of a reflection on the daffodil logo as a symbol of the hopefulness contained in the journey of loss.

Hope

The ground was cold and bare,
The bulbs, so brown and dull,
With hope were buried there,
As autumn came.
My life had lost its light;
My love was laid to rest;
I wept, in endless nights
And called your name.

The days grew long and sad.
Unseen, the bulbs lay dead
Like any hope I'd had,
In winter days,
My life, my routine hours,
My grind, my lifeless tasks,
My home, devoid of flowers
And sunshine rays.

The nights? Sleepless and dark.
The bulbs? Far from my thoughts,
For pain had left its mark
Now you had gone.
This life, a barren waste.

For what was sweet had died,
Leaving a bitter taste
To feed upon.

Old year gives birth to new.
Old bulbs have gone for good.
More days of missing you,
That's my New Year.
Old life is left behind.
New life? I don't yet know
When peace will fill my mind
And banish fear.

Old ways have had their time.
Old friends have come and gone.
Old words have lost their rhyme,
Old songs their tune.
New ways no purpose know.
New friendships, hard to form.
New words no comfort show.
Is it too soon –

Too soon to yet believe,
That life will bring again
A healing in my grief,
A hope that's mine?
My prayer, my endless plea,
My cry, my one desire,
Is that I yet might see
A rainbow sign.

Green shoots through dark earth rise.
The bulbs are breaking free,
And upwards turn their eyes
Towards the sun.
Are hopeful signs being given?

Will light defeat the dark?
Might hands reach up to heaven?
Can hell be shunned?

Green shoots of hope appear,
A smile, a moment free
Of pain and dull despair,
A glimpse of Spring.
Can hope bring life again?
Will purpose come from hope?
Might healing come from pain
And let me sing?

A bud can hold no more
The glory it contains,
The colour in its store,
Its treasure trove.
And hope will break its chains.
It must burst free and show
That death no victory gains
O'er life and love.

O grave, where is your sting
When bulbs burst forth with life,
And hope with triumph brings
New Life again?
Let me not doubt the growth
That hope will recreate
In barren, lifeless earth,
For me. Amen.

Travelling

I saw her come,
So weary from the journey,
alighting now into this unknown place,
not knowing where,
nor understanding why;
but now compelled
to take those faltering steps
and climb down from
the familiarity of what had been
her cocoon of safety,
her transport for her journey
for so long.

I saw her come,
and stand and look
upon this place of endings and beginnings,
this terminus and starting point,
this crossing of the routes
we all must take.

I saw her come,
relieved to have survived this ending,
yet fearful of this unknown place.

I saw her wait,
this frail survivor,
a waif-like traveller,
lost amongst the crowds who came and went;
so fearfully encumbered now
by all she had to gather up
and own, and safely keep;
an awkward rucksack –
(How can she hope to carry that?)

those spilling poly-bags –
(O why such chaos and disorder there as well?)
for this disorganised stranger.

I saw her wait
and gaze around with searching eyes,
with fear and hopelessness,
and questioning brow,
and hating this,
and hoping no one would notice.

I saw her wait,
and wonder in her waiting
what she must do.

I saw her go,
and gather up her complicated life,
and find a balance in the burdens
of her back and hands;
too frail,
too fragile, surely now, to move
with any strength and grace,
and find a way to go
with all her fearful load
of what she'd taken
on her journey to this unknown place,
for all her time of travelling.

I saw her go,
and lurch beneath the weight,
through crowds with equal loads,
and those with lighter step,
now bumped, now carrying on,
and, with resolve, to find her way.

I saw her go
and climb aboard another coach,
as I wondered at her going.

I saw her leave,
now settling with her burdens
spread around,
some lifted high,
some clutched as precious things;
a traveller travelling on,
with others in their place;
those strangers now
and yet companions too,
embarking on another travelling time,
a journey out and on
to who knows where?

I saw her leave,
and wondered how she'd be.
Would she remember what had been,
and value, even now,
the journey left behind
the tortuous travelling of the way she'd come?

I saw her leave,
and prayed for her beginning
and her journey through.

You live, you live

Dear God,
I live, and in my living,
live with death.
I live, they live,
They die, I die
and death is part of life.

My child,
you live, and in your living,
know of death.
You live, you live,
you die, you die,
and death and life are one.

So live,
and know that in your living,
life is real.
And know of death,
that it may speak to all your living,
of what is good,
and right,
and now.

Fourteen

Real people, real lives

'Some boys came out of a town and made fun of him. "Get out of here,
baldy!" they shouted.'
Bible: 2 Kings 2:23

'Will I be bald like you one day, daddy?'
James William Thomas Gordon, aged 7

It may come as a surprise to you find that I conclude this book by
telling you that my father began to lose his hair during the War when
he was in his early twenties. So, let me explain. Having become
engaged to my mother in 1940, the dashing Jimmy Gordon was
deeply worried that when the War ended she would no longer find
this demobbed airman fiancé returning home to the Highlands of
Scotland the blonde Adonis with wavy hair she had once known.
And so, as he confessed later, in the final months of his War service he
spent a fortune searching out and experimenting with a wide range of
patent hair-restoring remedies. None of them worked. As it turned
out, he needn't have worried. My mother loved him for what he was
and not for his hairstyle. They married in 1945, and their wedding
pictures contain the whole story – my mother a beauty with flowing
brunette locks, and my father a handsome-but-balding airman.

So, I had no chance. A sixties' teenager, my hair was my pride
and joy. The hairdryer and round curling-brush were essentials to
my manly accoutrements. My wedding photographs give proof that
I was one up on my father – no baldy, twenty-something stares back
at *me* from this 1974 wedding album! But alas, it was all pretence.
For, if I am to be honest, the onset of hair loss was well on its way
even by then. The inevitable could not be avoided. The fateful day

would not be far off. And so it was. Receding at the temples rapidly developed into a very high forehead. The expanding bald patch eventually linked up with the thinness at the front. I was indeed my father's son. And it would appear that James William Thomas Gordon, at the tender age of seven, realised he was my son too!

I have to say, though, that baldness hasn't really bothered me that much – though you wouldn't think so, would you, as I go on about it here? But, the fact is, I am what I am. And one part of me is my baldness. You just have to take it or leave it, for I can do nothing about it at all. I've never been teased much about my hair-loss. Oh, like most bald men I've had the odd quip about billiard balls and slap-heads and the like, and I've fended off further ribbing by joking about grass not growing on a busy street and levels of testosterone. But I have never been really ridiculed, and, as far as I can recall, I have never been called derogatory names – at least not to my face. But, if I had ... well ... who knows?

All of this gives me some insight into the psyche of Elisha the prophet, one of my own personal saints. The story of Elisha and Elijah is one of my favourite Bible tales[55]. Here's what it's about. Elijah had been a great prophet, one of the best. But now he had gone, carried in a whirlwind into heaven on a fiery chariot. Elisha was his protégé and chosen successor. So it was Elisha's job to get on with this prophet-of-God stuff. He had been groomed from the start, and was as well prepared for this prophet business as he could ever be. The 'mantle of Elijah' had fallen on his shoulders. OK so far? Fine! But then we have this bit at the end of this section of the story. Steel yourself ...

Elisha left Jericho to go to Bethel, and on the way some boys came out of a town and made fun of him. 'Get out of here, baldy!' they shouted. Elisha turned round, glared at them and cursed them in the name of the Lord. Then two she-bears came out of the woods and tore forty-two of the boys to pieces. Elisha went on to Mount Carmel and later returned to Samaria.

As if nothing out of the ordinary had happened, he went on to Mount Carmel and later returned to Samaria! Forty-two boys having a cheap laugh at a passing stranger, calling him names as he walked by, picking on his distinctive appearance; forty-two boys winding Elisha up because he was follically challenged; forty-two boys – or at least the bolder ones, the ringleaders, the toe-rags of their day – shouting, 'Get out of here, baldy! Baldy man! Baldy man! Ha, ha! Baldy, baldy!'; forty-two boys having a laugh at someone's else's expense. And forty-two boys now lying slaughtered, torn to pieces by two bears conjured up by this bald prophet – and in the name of the Lord to boot! And off Elisha goes, on to Mount Carmel, trotting up later to Samaria, quite the thing! He dusts his hands down, 'We'll have no more of that, thank you. Take that, you louts!' Zap! Wham! Kerpow! And off he strolls, quite jocko, as if nothing untoward had happened at all! That's that! And the incident never gets another mention.

Now, don't get me wrong, I love the Old Testament, with its vibrancy and vivid accounts of real events and real people. But, wow! When I first heard this story, I was terrified. As a wee boy in a strict Presbyterian churchgoing household, it didn't need any biblical exegesis of this passage to scare the life out of me! It did it all by itself. I fully identified with the forty-two youths. I'd had the odd bit of out-of-line behaviour myself, and I'd thought of plenty of names for odd-looking people, even if I hadn't shouted any of them out loud. But if this is the kind of punishment that powerful, God-fearing people like prophets – and, by implication, ministers and teachers and grandparents and dads and next-door neighbours and the local bobby and the like – can dole out at will, no wonder I had a passion about being a good boy. I didn't want the 1950s equivalent of two she-bears tearing me limb from limb, thank you very much. I will be good, I *will* – because I know what happens to boys who are not! *'For the Bible tells me so ...'*

Over the years the story of Elisha's massacre of the recalcitrant youths has troubled me as, indeed, have many difficult biblical passages about violence and retribution. Some of these I have wrestled with and come to rationalise and understand to my satisfaction. But this one ... well, it was just plain crazy, quite wrong, out of place in the pages of scripture. And I could do nothing more than dismiss it is an unfortunate intrusion and an unhelpful aberration.

That was until several years ago when, in a church service I was attending, one of the Bible readings was the account of the mantle of Elijah falling on Elisha, the role of prophet being passed on from one man to another, and the great prophet Elijah being taken up into heaven in his fiery chariot. It's a wonderful passage and one I knew well, and indeed one that I myself had preached on over the years. And it's the part of the Elijah and Elisha story which, I suspect, is most commonly known. But I have to confess, for one reason or another, my attention that day began to wander during the sermon, and my eye fell on the open Bible in front of me. I began to read further, beyond the bit we had already read, towards the end of the chapter. And there it was again, the massacre of the forty-two boys, the destructive retribution at the whim of the baldy Elisha. But this time the horrible events of this story would not go away. I was troubled to find this difficult passage once again, and I could not dismiss it from my mind. There must be a reason. There had to be a message somewhere hidden deep within these words. There had to be something being revealed here which was about Truth, and more, surely, than just the use of this story as an ultimate deterrent to scare wee boys of then and now into being good.

So over the next few weeks I struggled with this strange tale, its context, what preceded it and what followed, what other people had written about it, and much more. And eventually, a picture began to emerge. The story of Elijah and Elisha was about a relationship, a kind of father and son relationship, a colleague to colleague relationship, a mentor to student relationship, a leader to successor relationship.

However it is expressed, the unfolding story of Elisha puts him as close to Elijah as anyone could possibly be. And then the truth dawned! The story of the end of Elijah's life as one of glory and wonder, fiery chariots and the mantle falling on Elisha and all – good Cecil B De Mille stuff! – was not just about the transfer of power, title and responsibilities of a prophet as I had thought. It was about death and bereavement. It was about the intense struggle of a man to come to terms with the death of a loved one. And all the focus on the wonder and chariots and mantles and prophets had only served to mask the truth of that.

Elisha had lost the key person in his life, and as such he had lost his all. The context of my scary story was, therefore, loss. The background was about preparing to face that loss. What followed was the struggle of living with that loss. Elisha was a broken, bereaved man, and his loss was an enormous burden to carry. There was no getting away from that. And so it seemed to me, as a pragmatist rather than a biblical scholar, the story of the cursing of the forty-two boys was not a random inclusion, an aberration that didn't fit. It was, instead, part of that account, part of the unfolding story of a confused, devastated, bereaved man trying to make sense of the future without the man he loved and needed more than all else.

So Elisha was angry – a fearsome, lashing-out, irrational, don't-care-who-gets-in-the-way angry; an angry that I have seen in many other people since; an angry that makes no logical sense, and for many people, including, I suspect, Elisha himself, is absolutely out of character. So crippling, so disabling was his loss that anger was Elisha's overwhelming emotion. For him it happened to be bad boys who shouted 'Baldy, baldy' who got the full force of it. It could have been his granny, the next-door neighbour, a doctor, his minister, a bus driver, a shopkeeper, people laughing in Sainsbury's, the cat, the wall, the pillow, the door … It could have been anyone who simply looked at him the wrong way.

Now this weird story made sense to me. Through the eyes of my work as a hospice chaplain, because of my regular contact with bereaved people, and out of my increasing understanding of the bereavement journey, I could see the story of Elisha in the new way it speaks to me now. I now saw Elisha for what he was – a bereaved and broken man. And I saw the anger in the story of the cursing of the boys for what it was: a part of his journey of loss. I am still puzzled by the massacre of the boys. It seems such an over-the-top response in a Bible story. But that – for now at least – is no longer the point. For the issue that impacts on me now is Elisha's behaviour, his anger, his out-of-control approach to his bereavement. It cannot be right that he could call on his Lord to punish these boys in such a fashion. But it can be right and normal and predictable that, because of his loss, he could be angry enough to react like this. How do I know that? Because of what people tell me they feel like in their journeys of loss. And how do I know they are telling the truth? Because I have felt like that in my losses too.

So I'm grateful to the baldy Elisha for being a real person. I'm grateful that people like this are in the Bible because they make me feel normal, and not just because there's at least one man there who's as bald and me and my dad – and, ultimately, my own son – but because of the normal way he reacts to loss. And I'm grateful to the people I have worked with over the years who have now made the real Elisha come to life for me. For his was undoubtedly a bereavement journey, including his ferocious encounter with name-calling boys. That makes Elisha's story worth the reading, and seeing it for what it is.

'I swear by my loyalty to the Living Lord and to you that I will not leave you,' he tells Elijah, and there, in the depth of relationship, are Glenda and Steve. 'Yes I know, but don't let's talk about it,' he pleads with those who pointed to Elijah's impending death, and there, in the denial of reality, are Eddie and Peter. 'Let me receive a share of your power,' he asks of Elijah before he dies, and there, in the final moments, you find Edith and Brenda. 'That is a difficult request to grant,' Elijah tells him, and there, in promises which are hard to keep, emerge Charlie and Rita. 'Mighty defender of Israel, you are gone!' he cries in his loss, and there, out of control, is Tom Gordon when Talbot died. 'In his grief, Elisha tore his cloak in two,' we are told, and there, in a ritual act, you have Davy's funeral event. 'Where is the God of Elijah?' he prays, and there, in the struggle with faith, are Michael and Bob. 'The power of Elijah is on Elisha,' we are told, and there, in the burden of expectations, is Tom Gordon after the death of his mother. 'I have healed the water,' he affirms, and there, in the beginning of healing, you have Edith and Margo. 'He cursed them in the name of the Lord,' we read, and there, in the anger of loss, are Simon and Cindy. 'Elisha went on to Mount Carmel,' we are told, and there, in the beginning of new journeys, you find Hamish and Sue and Nellie.

Through it all, the balding, angry Elisha is a real man, with a real life, with a real loss to cope with, and with real feelings to show. That makes the story of Elisha worth the telling. And, if that is the case, it surely makes the stories of others in their losses worth the telling too. This is one normal person among many with stories to tell about their normal experiences of loss, about lessons learned, feelings shared and people helped. These are stories about how ordinary people become remarkable as they cope with the death of a loved one when they never thought they would ever be able to live again. Elisha became a remarkable man in his own right. His story, like those this book contains, is ultimately about hope and purpose. His story, with the others, is all about me and all about you.

William Gladstone, in his speech on the Reform Bill in 1866, said, 'You cannot fight against the future. Time is on our side.' When real people live real lives and cope with real losses, they, like all of us, cannot fight against the future either. There is a life out there to face and to make sense of as best we can. There is a future which we have to face no matter what. And, of course, we have to struggle with real feelings of giving up on that future, because the journey into it is hellish and what awaits us there is something we neither expected nor want to deal with. But if we have anything, we have time. We have time when every second in the journey of loss seems an eternity, and the passing of eons of time takes us no distance at all from the reality of loss. We have all the time we need. So don't hurry with your journey. And don't rush other people along through their grief. Be patient with yourself and with others. Let patience be your constant companion. And when you lose that patience, wait a while till it returns.

The reality is that with time on our side there will be many real and varied situations to face. There will be times of questioning, when, with all normality gone, there are anxieties about how we cope with unfamiliar structures and learn new ways. I spoke with Theo recently about how he was coping some years now after his wife's death. 'Aye, the wife'll be proud of me,' he said, 'for I've got to be a real expert at my dobying …' Now, this wasn't a word I'd heard before – and I'm not even sure I have spelled it correctly here – so I asked Theo what he meant. 'Oh, dobying,' he replied, 'that's doing your washing, your clothes and stuff. It comes from the navy. I did my own dobying when I was at sea with the Merchant Navy. But all my married life the wife did it for me. When she died, I didn't know where to start. But I had to learn, didn't I? After a fortnight I'd run out of shirts to wear. So I had to dig out the instruction book for the washing machine and get started. I was cursing the wife for not being there, and cursing the washing machine people for preparing an instruction booklet that only women could understand. But I got there, right enough. Now I'm a dobying expert. See! Don't you like the shirt?'

Theo had new roles to take on. Unwilling, unready, he had to face the fact that without his wife he had new things to learn, or else he wouldn't have survived. When my mother died, my father couldn't boil an egg. But he learned, he had to, and he became the best home-made-soup maker in the street. There's hope for us all!

Three times a year, in January, May and September, on a Sunday afternoon, we invite people back to the hospice for what we call 'A time to remember'. Through appropriate music and guided by suitable readings, those who come and share in the restful environment of our day centre take time to remember. On each occasion, during a reflective piece of music, people are invited to come to the table at the front to lay there a little card on which they have written the name of the person they have come to remember. It's often a tearful occasion and the boxes of tissues strategically placed around the room are well used. But these times to remember have come to be very important in our bereavement support work, simply because they allow people to know that, whatever time it takes, and however long it has been since their loss, their remembrances are still so very important.

There are a number of things that always strike us as significant on these occasions. People never rush to leave; they stay for tea and coffee and they talk, and sometimes they share with people they have never met before how they are coping with their loss. Then there are the people who come back ages after a death, reminding us that while the world has moved on and has largely forgotten about their loss, they are still living with it, and it's as real in their lives as it ever was. So they need to mark it, have it acknowledged in some way and with some purpose once again. But perhaps the most significant aspect of these gatherings is that there are more names on the remembrance cards than there are people attending the event. The people there have been invited to a time of remembrance because they have had a bereavement in the hospice's circle of care. But they have other names to remember too, parents, grandparents, friends, relations, folk from recent memory and folk from long ago. So there are many

names on the cards, names of people we have never heard of before.
Should that be surprising? I hope not. For just as one death trig-
gers off memories of others who have died, so one event brings back
countless memories of special people over a long, long time. Tearful?
Of course. Helpful? Profoundly so. And maybe it's even a reminder
of our own mortality, and that one day people might remember us in
like fashion.

James Keelaghan is right. 'Everyone dies.' (See Ch. 6) The fact of
birth brings with it the inevitability of death. There is no escaping
that. It is the given. The trouble is that most of us most of the time
live in denial of the reality of our own mortality, so that when we are
faced with it or when we see our mortality staring back at us in the
death of a loved one, we do not know where to begin. It's not that
we should live in a morbid state, thinking about the reality of death in
our every waking moment, or, like my lovely grandmother, choose
not to talk about death in case it makes it happen quicker! It's just that
living with our mortality would perhaps make us deal with some of
the bigger issues of life before it is too late to do anything about it.

My friend Zam Walker, one of those with whom I shared the
'Living with cancer' week on Iona, was told she had breast cancer
and had to have a radical mastectomy right away and be faced with
radiotherapy and chemotherapy thereafter. She had two years of hell.
Thankfully, she came through that, and she is now, she tells me, a
wiser person, a deeper thinker, and someone who has come to
appreciate the preciousness of life every day, because she almost lost
it altogether. However, she puts her learning in a more challenging
way. She does not say, 'This is a good day to be alive,' as if in some
fashion she has won a victory over death and staved off the grim
reaper for a while longer. Instead, with the wisdom of the ancients in
their spiritual journey, she says, 'This is a good day to die.' And in so
doing she is seeking in herself some completeness in her living, and
seeking in her relationships with family and friends some complete-

ness to her loving. Her membership of the 'cancer club' has made her face her mortality. She feels she has to do that every day in order really to appreciate the value of living.

John Bell and the Wild Goose Resource Group offer us this meditation on the reality of living with our dying:[56]

I never wanted to be born.

The older I grew
the fonder I became
of my mother's womb
and its warmth and safety.

I feared the unknown:
 the next world,
about which I knew nothing
but imagined the worst.

Yet, as I grew older
I sensed in my soul
that the womb was not my home for ever.

Though I did not know when,
I felt that one day
I would disappear through a door
which had yet to be opened,
and confront the unknown
of which I was afraid.

And then,
it happened.

In blood, tears and pain
it happened.

I was cut off from the familiar;
I left my life behind
and discovered not darkness, but light,
not hostility but love,
not eternal separation
but hands that wanted to hold me.

I never wanted to be born.

I don't want to die.

The older I grow,
the fonder I become
of this world
and its warmth and safety.

I fear the unknown:
  the next world,
about which I know nothing
but imagine the worst.

Yet, as I grow older
I sense in my soul
that this world is not my home for ever.

Though I do not know when,
I feel that one day
I will disappear through a door
which has yet to be opened.

Perhaps having come so safely through the first door
I should not fear so hopelessly the second.

Real people live real lives. Real lives will bring real losses and real feelings. Real journeys of grief will bring real pain and real hope. So, let reality speak to us, and let these real people have their experiences affirmed and their voices heard. And let them accompany you, the real people that you are, as your new journeys now begin.

Notes

56 From *He Was In the World: Meditations for public worship*, John L. Bell, published by Wild Goose Publications, 1995, ISBN 0 947988 70 X.

Be real

Be real, and not pretend.
Do right, and do not spend
Your time being what you're not.
Be what you are, and know
Being real's the way to go.
In fact, it's all you've got.

Be true to what you are,
Ev'n if being true's by far
The hardest thing to do,
When others put you down,
And there's no one around
Who might believe in you.

Be real – try not to hide
The 'I' that's deep inside,
That's been there from the start,
The essence you can find,
Your being, soul, or mind,
What matters most – your heart.

Be true when you need most
The confidence you've lost,
And tried so hard to save.
When faith in self has gone,
Believe you've been loved from
The cradle to the grave.

Be real, be you, OK?
For you were made that way,
Child of eternity,
Unique in time and space,
A product of God's grace,
You matter. Don't you see?

Be true to what you know,
Ev'n when the 'me' you show's
Not what you want to be.
So love yourself, and hear,
This whisper in your ear,
'You're loved by God and me.'

A carer's prayer

Jesus said:
Come unto me all who labour and are heavy laden,
and I will give you rest.

My God,
you told me 'Bid them come.'
So I said 'Come!'
to needy pilgrims on the weary way of life.
I promised them,
that in your name and in your strength
I would now offer help and healing,
and offer love
and offer me.

My God!
You said 'It's now.'
And so I opened up my heart,
my home,
the inner places of my very soul.
For now the time was right,
as one by weary one
the pilgrims came
and filled my love with need.

My God,
My God of life and love,
your gentle voice said:
'Turn not one away.'
And so another came,
and yet one more,
and others with them forced their way,
all those
who'd been concealed behind the first

slipped in along with them
and filled the very corners
of the space that once was mine.

My God,
please bid them go,
and let me know
some space and time and peace again.
I promise them,
I promise you
there will be other times
when I'll say 'Come.'
But in this moment
give me rest and peace.
For I've not love enough for this.
I did not know
so many weary ones would come my way.

'My child,' I hear God say,
'my friend,
my servant now,
I bid you come,
for did you not believe that you,
a weary pilgrim too,
could come and rest in me?'
'It's now,' my God will say,
'for you to know my heart,
my home,
my love
has plenty space for you –
and you –
and you.

'I am your life,' I hear again.
'I am your love.
So rest a while
as others come to me.
And know that when you turn away from weary ones
and rest in me,
you do not fail their need or mine.
So look!
You also cause those pilgrims now to turn
and in your open heart
and home
and soul
to know what's mine alone to give,
a greater rest in me
for pilgrims on the weary way of life
that they –
and you –
must know.'

My song, my life

My song, unsung; its words
as yet unformed;
its form an unknown thing;
its notes unclear.
No one can learn
its melody and sing.
My song, unborn,
lies still, its cry unheard.

My song of life, unknown.
My days appear,
devoid of clarity.
What purpose now
can fill the void
I feel, and set me free
from days of fear
and sorrow's piteous moan?

My song, so good to hear,
so rich with form,
once soared on heaven's wings;
with purpose filled,
with tune to touch
the heart and make it sing;
when hope was stirred
again, and love was near.

My song of life, so dear
and once so warm,
becomes this shapeless thing
I do not know

or recognise
as mine. How can I sing
and yet adorn
this life, so dead, so drear?

My song I'll write again,
await the muse
and shape the notes once more.
I'll pen my rhymes;
into new lines
I'll all my sorrows pour,
never to lose
my grasp on love's refrain.

My life is not in vain.
I'll find a way
to shape my days once more
into a life
where voices rise
and up to heaven soar;
my song reborn,
my Love to sing again.

The Iona Community is:

- An ecumenical movement of men and women from different walks of life and different traditions in the Christian church
- Committed to the gospel of Jesus Christ, and to following where that leads, even into the unknown
- Engaged together, and with people of goodwill across the world, in acting, reflecting and praying for justice, peace and the integrity of creation
- Convinced that the inclusive community we seek must be embodied in the community we practise

Together with our staff, we are responsible for:

- Our islands residential centres of Iona Abbey, the MacLeod Centre on Iona, and Camas Adventure Centre on the Ross of Mull

and in Glasgow:

- The administration of the Community
- Our work with young people
- Our publishing house, Wild Goose Publications
- Our association in the revitalising of worship with the Wild Goose Resource Group

The Iona Community was founded in Glasgow in 1938 by George MacLeod, minister, visionary and prophetic witness for peace, in the context of the poverty and despair of the Depression. Its original task of rebuilding the monastic ruins of Iona Abbey became a sign of hopeful rebuilding of community in Scotland and beyond. Today, we are about 250 Members, mostly in Britain, and 1500 Associate Members, with 1400 Friends worldwide. Together and apart, 'we follow the light we have, and pray for more light'.

For information on the Iona Community contact: The Iona Community, Fourth Floor, Savoy House, 140 Sauchiehall Street, Glasgow G2 3DH, UK. Phone: 0141 332 6343
e-mail: ionacomm@gla.iona.org.uk; web: www.iona.org.uk

For enquiries about visiting Iona, please contact: Iona Abbey, Isle of Iona, Argyll PA76 6SN, UK. Phone: 01681 700404
e-mail: ionacomm@iona.org.uk